EYEWITNESS *Travel* *Guides*

THAI
PHRASE BOOK

DK PUBLISHING, INC.
www.dk.com

A DK PUBLISHING BOOK

Compiled by Lexus Ltd with David and Somsong Smyth

First American Edition, 1998
2 4 6 8 10 9 7 5 3 1

Published in the United States by DK Publishing, Inc.
95 Madison Avenue, New York, New York 10016
Visit us on the World Wide Web at www.dk.com

Library of Congress Cataloging-in-Publication Data
Thai. -- 1st American ed.
    p.   cm. -- (Eyewitness travel guide phrase books)
    ISBN 0–7894–3593–4
    1. Thai language--Conversation and phrase books--English.
I. DK Publishing, Inc. II. Series.
PL4163.T475 1998
495.9'183421--DC21   98–18241
                                                CIP

Picture Credits
Jacket: All special photography DK Studio; Stewart Isset;
Clive Streeter

Printed and bound in Italy by Printer Trento Srl.

CONTENTS

PREFACE

This *Eyewitness Travel Guide Phrase Book* has been compiled
by experts to meet the general needs of tourists and business
travelers. Arranged under headings such as Hotels, Driving,
and so forth, the ample selection of useful words and phrases is
shown with an easy-to-follow system of imitated pronunciation,
as well as Thai characters. Although plenty of help is given
regarding pronunciation (see pages 5–6), there are—as in
Chinese—some tricky tones to master. If you feel unsure of
yourself, simply point to the phrase you want to say.

  Typical replies to questions you may ask during your trip, and
the signs or instructions you may see or hear, are shown in
tinted boxes headed *Things You'll Hear* and *Things You'll See*.

  A 1,200-line mini-dictionary will help you form additional
phrases (or at least express the one word you need), and the
extensive menu guide will ease your way through complicated
Thai meals. In the Cross-cultural Notes section you will find
guidance on aspects of the Thai way of life. An understanding
of customs and points of etiquette will greatly enhance your
trip to Thailand, and your hosts will appreciate the effort you
have made to respect their culture and to speak their language.

Eyewitness Travel Guides are recognized as the world's best
travel guides. Each title features specially commissioned color
photographs, cutaways of major buildings, 3-D aerial views,
and detailed maps, plus information on sights, events, hotels,
restaurants, shopping, and entertainment.

Eyewitness Travel Guides titles include:
Thailand · Amsterdam · Australia · Sydney · California · Florida
Hawaii · New York · San Francisco & Northern California · France
Loire Valley · Paris · Provence · Great Britain · London · Ireland
Greece: Athens & the Mainland · The Greek Islands · Istanbul
Italy · Florence & Tuscany · Naples · Rome · Venice & the Veneto
Moscow · St Petersburg · Portugal · Lisbon · Prague · Sardinia
Spain · Seville & Andalusia · Vienna · Warsaw

PRONUNCIATION

When reading the imitated pronunciation, pronounce each
syllable as if it formed part of an English word and you will be
understood fairly well. Remember the points below and your
pronunciation will be even closer to the correct Thai.

a	as in "ago"
e	as in "hen"
i	as in "thin"
o	as in "on"
u	as in "gun"
ah	as in "rather"
ai	as in "Thai"
air	as in "pair"
ao	as in "Mao Tse-Tung"
ay	as in "day"
ee	as in "see"
er	as in "enter"
er-ee	(don't pronounce the "r")
eu	as in a sound of disgust that a comic might write as "errgh"
ew	as in "few"
oh	as in "go"
oo	as in "boot"
OO	as in "book"
oy	as in "toy"
bp	between a "b" and a "p"—not a double sound
dt	between a "d" and a "t"—not a double sound
g	as in "give"
j	as in "jet"
ng	as in "sing"

When **p**, **t**, or **k** occur at the end of words in Thai, the sound is
"swallowed" or "not released."

Note that many Thais have difficulty pronouncing "r" sounds and will substitute an "l"; thus **a-rai** ("What?") becomes **a-lai**.

TONES

Thai is a tonal language. This means that the pitch at which a syllable is pronounced determines its meaning. Thus, the word **mâi**, pronounced with a falling intonation, means "not," but the word **măi**, pronounced with a rising intonation, means "silk."

There are five tones in Thai:

mid-tone	no symbol
falling tone	ˆ
rising tone	ˇ
high tone	´
low tone	`

Mid-tone: this is similar to the normal pitch of voice.

Falling tone: this can be thought of as similar to an emphatic pronunciation in English as, for example, when repeating a word a number of times over the telephone.

Rising tone: this is similar to a questioning intonation.

High tone: this is pitched slightly higher than normal.

Low tone: this is pitched slightly lower than normal.

MALE/FEMALE

The forms **kâ**, **dee-chún**, and **chún** given in parentheses replace the preceding word and are used by female speakers. For example, **kOOn krúp** (**ka**): **kOOn krúp** is used by a man and **kOOn kâ** by a woman.

CROSS-CULTURAL NOTES

Visitors to Thailand are always impressed by the warmth, friendliness, and tolerance of Thai people. Nevertheless, there are certain important do's and don'ts that the visitor should observe so as not to cause offense.

THE MONARCHY

The monarchy is highly revered in Thailand. Criticism of the institution or members of the royal family, whether real or imagined, is deeply offensive to most Thais and can lead to serious trouble. Few Thais would wish to discuss seriously anything to do with the monarchy with a foreign visitor, and these feelings should be respected.

RELIGION

Temples, Buddha images, and monks should all be treated with appropriate respect. Shoes should be removed in certain parts of the temple, and any restrictions on taking photographs should be observed. Kneel or sit cross-legged in the main hall of a temple, to make sure that your feet are not pointing toward the Buddha image. Monks are strictly forbidden to have any physical contact with women, so female visitors should make certain that they do not accidentally come into close contact with a monk. It is perfectly acceptable, however, to speak to a monk, especially if you have questions about Buddhism.

APPEARANCES

In Thailand people are judged very much by their appearance, and most Thais invest considerable time, effort, and money in order to look good. As a result, they cannot help but look askance at the sometimes rather sloppily attired Western visitors they see. While they will generally be much too polite to say what they think directly, the warning notices in many temples refusing admission to unacceptably dressed visitors reflect the disapproval that Thais instinctively feel. So, if you are meeting Thai friends or visiting them at their homes, it is good manners to make an effort to look respectable, even if this means erring on the conservative side in your style of dress.

MEETING THAI PEOPLE

You should address Thais who are of similar age or older than you are by using the polite title **kOOn** in front of their first name, regardless of whether you are speaking to a man or a woman. Thus Mr. Somchai Sombatcharoen would be addressed (and referred to) as **KOOn Somchai** and Mrs. Nuantip Bunsin as **KOOn Nuantip**.

If you are invited to a Thai home, remember to take your shoes off just before entering the house. Members of the household will probably greet you with a **wai**—a gesture of both greeting and respect in which the hands are held together in a prayer-like position in front of the face—which should be returned. The fingertips should be nearer the forehead when making a **wai** to people of equal or superior status and nearer the chin when responding to the **wai** of children or those of inferior status. Thais also show respect to older or more senior people by trying to keep their head at a lower level when passing by them or talking to them. While this custom does not have to be observed too literally, it is, for example, a mark of good manners to make an obvious gesture of bending forward a little when passing elderly members of the household who are seated.

When Thais meet casually or by chance, they will often greet each other with the question **bpai nǎi?** ("where are you going?") or **bpai nǎi mah?** ("where have you been?"). This is usually more an informal greeting than an attempt to find out about their friend's immediate destination or recent whereabouts. A rather vague answer, such as **bpai têe-o** ("I'm going out") or **bpai têe-o mah** ("I've been out"), is a perfectly acceptable response.

Surface Harmony

In Thailand the preservation of surface harmony is considered of the utmost importance. Losing one's temper, arguing, and direct criticism of others are regarded as threats to such harmony and are consequently frowned upon.

Personal Conduct

Westerners can unintentionally cause offense by pointing at things with their foot, by sitting in such a way that their feet are pointing at a Thai, and by touching or patting Thais on the head. Such actions will cause Thais considerable discomfort even if they are too polite to say so. Many of Bangkok's long-suffering **samlor** drivers sit silently fuming while thoughtless tourists rest their feet on the rail behind the driver's seat, only inches from his head.

Displaying physical affection in public toward a member of the opposite sex is also frowned upon by many Thais, although in recent years it has become more common to see young couples in Bangkok holding hands. Physical contact between friends of the same sex, however, is perfectly acceptable, and it is not uncommon to see young men or women walking hand in hand with a friend of the same sex.

Polite Language

An important way of expressing politeness when speaking Thai is to use a polite particle—a word for which there is no equivalent in English—at the end of a sentence. Thus, men will add the word **krúp** at the end of both statements and questions in order to sound more polite, and women will say **ká** at the end of questions and **kâ** at the end of statements. While these particles have generally been omitted in the phrases given in this book, you are advised to add them to the end of every phrase at first, on the grounds that it is generally better to sound too polite than not polite enough. Gradually you will learn when it is appropriate to use them.

USEFUL EVERYDAY PHRASES

Yes/No
châi/mâi châi
ใช่ / ไม่ใช่
or
krúp (kâ)/mâi krúp (kâ)
ครับ (ค่ะ) / ไม่ครับ (ค่ะ)

There are no single words for "yes" or "no" in Thai. The appropriate word depends on the way in which the question is phrased. Generally, to answer "yes" to a question, the verb in the question is repeated; to say "no," the negative word **mâi** is used in front of the verb. Since questions are often phrased in the form of a statement followed by . . . **châi mái** ("isn't that so?"), the word **châi** is often thought of as being equivalent to "yes" and **mâi châi** equivalent to "no." In addition, the polite particles **krúp** (spoken by men) and **kâ** (spoken by women) are also used to mean "yes," and **mâi krúp (kâ)** to mean "no."

Thank you/No, thank you
kòrp-kOOn/mâi ao kòrp-kOOn
ขอบคุณ / ไม่เอาขอบคุณ

Please (*offering*)
chern krúp (kâ)
เชิญครับ (ค่ะ)

Please (*asking for something*)
kŏr . . .
ขอ ...

Please (*asking someone to do something*)
chôo-ay . . .
ช่วย ...

I don't understand
mâi kâo-jai
ไม่เข้าใจ

Do you speak English?
pôot pah-săh ung-grìt bpen mái?
พูดภาษาอังกฤษเป็นไหม

I can't speak Thai
pôot pah-săh tai mâi bpen
พูดภาษาไทยไม่เป็น

I don't know
mâi sâhp
ไม่ทราบ

Please speak more slowly
chôo-ay pôot cháh cháh nòy dâi mái
ช่วยพูดช้าๆหน่อยได้ไหม

Please write it down for me
chôo-ay kĕe-un long hâi nòy dâi mái?
ช่วยเขียนลงให้หน่อยได้ไหม

My name is . . .
pŏm (dee-chún) chêu . . .
ผม (ดิฉัน) ชื่อ ...

How do you do, pleased to meet you
sa-wùt dee krúp (kâ), yin dee têe dâi róo-jùk
สวัสดีครับ (ค่ะ) ยินดีที่ได้รู้จัก

Good morning/afternoon/evening
sa-wùt dee krúp (kâ)
สวัสดีครับ (ค่ะ)

Good-bye
lah gòrn ná
ลาก่อนนะ

How are you?
bpen yung-rai bâhng? / sa-bai dee réu?
เป็นอย่างไรบ้าง / สบายดีหรือ

Excuse me, please
kŏr-tôht krúp (kâ)
ขอโทษครับ (ค่ะ)

Sorry!
kŏr-tôht krúp (kâ)
ขอโทษครับ (ค่ะ)

I'm really sorry
pŏm (dee-chún) sĕe-a jai jing jing
ผม (ดิฉัน) เสียใจจริงๆ

Can you help me?
chôo-ay pŏm (dee-chún) nòy dâi mái?
ช่วยผม (ดิฉัน) หน่อยได้ไหม

Can I have . . . ?
kŏr . . .
ขอ ...

I would like . . .
ao/yahk dai . . .
เอา / อยากได้ ...

Is there . . . here?
têe-nêe mee . . . mái?
ที่นี่มี ... ไหม

Where can I get . . . ?
séu . . . dâi têe-nǎi?
ซื้อ ... ได้ที่ไหน

How much is it?
tâo-rài krúp (ká)?
เท่าไรครับ (คะ)

What time is it?
gèe mohng láir-o?
กี่โมงแล้ว

I must go now
dtôrng bpai la
ต้องไปละ

I'm lost
pǒm (dee-chún) lǒng tahng
ผม (ดิฉัน) หลงทาง

Do you take credit cards?
têe-nêe rúp bùt kray-dìt mái?
ที่นี่รับบัตรเครดิตไหม

Where is the restroom?
hôrng náhm yòo têe-nǎi?
ห้องน้ำอยู่ที่ไหน

Go away!
bpai hâi pón!
ไปให้พัน

Excellent!
yêe-um ler-ee!
เยี่ยมเลย

THINGS YOU'LL SEE

ปิด	**bpìt**	closed
ลิฟท์	**líf**	elevator
ทางเข้า	**tahng kâo**	entrance
ทางออก	**tahng òrk**	exit
ให้เช่า	**hâi châo**	for rent
ขาย	**kăi**	for sale
สุภาพบุรุษ	**sOO-pâhp bOO-ròOt**	men
ชาย	**chai**	men
ช.		men
ห้ามเข้า	**hâhm kâo**	no entrance
ห้ามสูบบุหรี่	**hâhm sòop bOO-rèe**	no smoking
ไม่ว่าง	**mâi wâhng**	occupied
เปิด	**bpèrt**	open
เปิดเวลา	**bpèrt way-lah**	opening times
ดึง	**deung**	pull
ผลัก	**plùk**	push
สุขา	**sÒO-kăh**	restroom
ห้องน้ำ	**hôrng náhm**	restroom
ลดราคา	**lót rah-kah**	sale
เงียบ	**ngêe-up**	silence, quiet
หญิง	**yĭng**	women
ญ.		women
สุภาพสตรี	**sOO-pâhp sa-dtree**	women

14

THINGS YOU'LL HEAR

a-rai ná?	Excuse me?
bpen yung-rai bâhng?	How are you?
dĕe-o póp gun mài	See you later
kòrp-kOOn	Thanks
kŏr tôht	Excuse me
lah gòrn ná	Good-bye
mâi bpen rai	You're welcome; Never mind
mâi kâo jai	I don't understand
mâi sâhp/róo	I don't know
nêe ngai lâ	Here you are
ra-wung!	Look out!
rĕu/lĕr krúp (ká)?	Is that so?
sa-bai dee krúp (kâ)	Very well, thank you
—láir-o kOOn lâ	—and you?
sa-wùt dee krúp (kâ)	Good-bye
sa-wùt dee krúp (kâ)	How do you do, nice to
yin dee têe dâi	meet you
róo-jùk gun	
tòok láir-o	That's right

DAYS, MONTHS, SEASONS

Sunday	wun ah-tít	วันอาทิตย์
Monday	wun jun	วันจันทร์
Tuesday	wun ung-kahn	วันอังคาร
Wednesday	wun pÓOt	วันพุธ
Thursday	wun pa-réu-hùt	วันพฤหัส
Friday	wun sÒOk	วันศุกร์
Saturday	wun săo	วันเสาร์

January	mók-ga-rah-kom	มกราคม
February	gOOm-pah-pun	กุมภาพันธ์
March	mee-nah-kom	มีนาคม
April	may-săh-yon	เมษายน
May	préut-sa-pah-kom	พฤษภาคม
June	mí-tOO-nah-yon	มิถุนายน
July	ga-rúk-ga-dah-kom	กรกฎาคม
August	sĭng-hăh-kom	สิงหาคม
September	gun-yah-yon	กันยายน
October	dtOO-lah-kom	ตุลาคม
November	préut-sa-jik-gah-yon	พฤศจิกายน
December	tun-wah-kom	ธันวาคม

Spring	réu-doo bai-mái plì	ฤดูใบไม้ผลิ
Summer	réu-doo rórn	ฤดูร้อน
Autumn	réu-doo bai-mái rôo-ung	ฤดูใบไม้ร่วง
Winter	réu-doo năo	ฤดูหนาว

cool season *(Nov-Feb)*	nâh năo	หน้าหนาว
hot season *(Mar-June)*	nâh rórn	หน้าร้อน
rainy season *(Jul-Oct)*	nâh fŏn	หน้าฝน
Christmas	krít-sa-maht	คริสต์มาส
New Year	bpee mài	ปีใหม่
New Year's Eve	wun sîn bpee	วันสิ้นปี
Thai New Year *(April)*	sŏng-grahn	สงกรานต์
Chinese New Year	dtròOt jeen	ตรุษจีน

NUMBERS

In Thai script the first item is the numeral and the second the word.

0	sŏon	๐	ศูนย์
1	nèung	๑	หนึ่ง
2	sŏrng	๒	สอง
3	săhm	๓	สาม
4	sèe	๔	สี่
5	hâh	๕	ห้า
6	hòk	๖	หก
7	jèt	๗	เจ็ด
8	bpàirt	๘	แปด
9	gâo	๙	เก้า
10	sìp	๑๐	สิบ
11	sìp-èt	๑๑	สิบเอ็ด
12	sìp-sŏrng	๑๒	สิบสอง
13	sìp-săhm	๑๓	สิบสาม
14	sìp-sèe	๑๔	สิบสี่
15	sìp-hâh	๑๕	สิบห้า
16	sìp-hòk	๑๖	สิบหก
17	sìp-jèt	๑๗	สิบเจ็ด
18	sìp-bpàirt	๑๘	สิบแปด
19	sìp-gâo	๑๙	สิบเก้า
20	yêe-sìp	๒๐	ยี่สิบ
21	yêe-sìp-èt	๒๑	ยี่สิบเอ็ด
22	yêe-sìp-sŏrng	๒๒	ยี่สิบสอง

30	săhm-sìp	๓๐	สามสิบ
31	săhm-sìp-èt	๓๑	สามสิบเอ็ด
32	săhm-sìp sŏrng	๓๒	สามสิบสอง
40	sèe-sìp	๔๐	สี่สิบ
50	hâh-sìp	๕๐	ห้าสิบ
60	hòk-sìp	๖๐	หกสิบ
70	jèt-sìp	๗๐	เจ็ดสิบ
80	bpàirt-sìp	๘๐	แปดสิบ
90	gâo-sìp	๙๐	เก้าสิบ
100	nèung róy	๑๐๐	หนึ่งร้อย
101	nèung róy nèung	๑๐๑	หนึ่งร้อยหนึ่ง
110	nèung róy sìp	๑๑๐	หนึ่งร้อยสิบ
200	sŏrng róy	๒๐๐	สองร้อย
300	săhm róy	๓๐๐	สามร้อย
400	sèe róy	๔๐๐	สี่ร้อย
1,000	nèung pun	๑๐๐๐	หนึ่งพัน
10,000	nèung mèun	๑๐๐๐๐	หนึ่งหมื่น
20,000	sŏrng mèun	๒๐๐๐๐	สองหมื่น
100,000	nèung săirn	๑๐๐๐๐๐	หนึ่งแสน
1,000,000	nèung láhn	๑๐๐๐๐๐๐	หนึ่งล้าน

COUNTING

When using number words with nouns, Thai also uses *classifiers*. Sometimes these are similar to English; for example:

two bowls of egg noodles
ba-mèe sŏrng chahm
egg noodles—two—bowls

three bottles of beer
bee-a sǎhm kòo-ut
beer—three—bottles

The words "bowls" and "bottles" in these phrases act like classifiers in Thai. But, whereas English uses these classifier-like words only in certain cases, Thai always needs a classifier with a noun:

three tickets
dtǒo-a sǎhm bai
ticket—three—classifier for tickets

two cars
rót sŏrng kun
car—two—classifier for vehicles

The words **bai** and **kun** in these examples are classifiers that have no equivalent in the English translations.

The counting word comes before the classifier unless only one object is being referred to, in which case the word for "one" comes after the classifier:

one/a coffee
gah-fair tôo-ay nèung
coffee—cup—one

one/a friend
pêu-un kon nèung
friend—classifier—one

The most common classifiers are:

kon	people (other than monks and royalty)
kun	vehicles
cha-bùp	letters, newspapers, documents
chín	pieces of things, such as cake, meat, cloth, etc.
dtoo-a	animals
bai	fruit, eggs, leaves, items of dishes, slips of paper
lêm	books, knives
lŭng	houses
lôok	fruit, balls
hôrng	rooms
hàirng	places
un	things—a general classifier that can be used for counting inanimate things when you can't remember the correct classifier.

The words for various units of time and measure behave like classifiers:

three days
sǎhm wun

five kilometers
hâh gi-loh-mét

one year
bpee nèung

one kilo
gi-loh nèung

TIME AND THE CALENDAR

today	wun née	วันนี้
yesterday	mêu-a wahn née	เมื่อวานนี้
tomorrow	prôОng née	พรุ่งนี้
the day before yesterday	wun seun née	วันซืนนี้
the day after tomorrow	wun ma-reun née	วันมะรืนนี้
this week	ah-tít née	อาทิตย์นี้
last week	ah-tít gòrn	อาทิตย์ก่อน
next week	ah-tít nâh	อาทิตย์หน้า
this morning	cháo née	เช้านี้
this afternoon	bài née	บ่ายนี้
this evening	yen née	เย็นนี้
tonight	keun née	คืนนี้
yesterday afternoon	bài wahn née	บ่ายวานนี้
last night	mêu-a keun née	เมื่อคืนนี้
tomorrow morning	prôОng née cháo	พรุ่งนี้เช้า
tomorrow night	prôОng née glahng keun	พรุ่งนี้กลางคืน
in three days	èek săhm wun	อีกสามวัน
three days ago	săhm wun gòrn	สามวันก่อน
late	cháh	ช้า
early	ray-o	เร็ว
soon	nai mâi cháh	ในไม่ช้า
later on	tee lŭng	ทีหลัง
at the moment	dĕe-o née	เดี๋ยวนี้
second	wí-nah-tee	วินาที

minute	nah-tee	นาที
one minute	nèung nah-tee	หนึ่งนาที
two minutes	sŏrng nah-tee	สองนาที
quarter of an hour	sìp-hâh nah-tee	สิบห้านาที
half an hour	krêung chôo-a mohng	ครึ่งชั่วโมง
three quarters of an hour	sèe sìp-hâh nah-tee	สี่สิบห้านาที
hour	chôo-a mohng	ชั่วโมง
that day	wun nún	วันนั้น
every day	tóOk wun	ทุกวัน
all day	túng wun	ทั้งวัน
the next day	wun rôOng kêun	วันรุ่งขึ้น

TELLING TIME

In the Thai system of telling time the day is divided into four sections of six hours. Thus, 7 AM reverts to "one o'clock," 8 AM to "two o'clock," and so on until noon. The same pattern is repeated in the second half of the day with 7 PM becoming "one o'clock," 8 PM "two o'clock," and so on. Each six hour period (and the hours from 5 PM to 6 PM) is known by a different name that is used when telling the time:

dtee	1 AM to 5 AM	**yen**	5 PM to 6 PM
cháo	6 AM to 11 AM	**tÔOm**	7 PM to midnight
bài	1 PM to 4 PM		

The 24 hours of the day are expressed as follows:

midnight	têe-ung keun	**5** AM	dtee hâh
1 AM	dtee nèung	**6** AM	hòk mohng cháo
2 AM	dtee sŏrng	**7** AM	jèt mohng cháo
3 AM	dtee săhm	*or*	mohng cháo
4 AM	dtee sèe	**8** AM	sŏrng mohng cháo

9 AM	sǎhm mohng cháo	5 PM	hâh mohng yen
10 AM	sèe mohng cháo	6 PM	hòk mohng yen
11 AM	hâh mohng cháo	7 PM	tÔOm nèung
noon	têe-ung wun	8 PM	sǒrng tÔOm
1 PM	bài mohng	9 PM	sǎhm tÔOm
2 PM	bài sǒrng mohng	10 PM	sèe tÔOm
3 PM	bài sǎhm mohng	11 PM	hâh tÔOm
4 PM	bài sèe mohng		

The word for "half" is **krêung**, which is added to the hour; minutes past the hour are expressed in the form: hour—number of minutes—**nah-tee** ("minute"), while minutes to the hour are expressed as **èek** ("further")—number of minutes—**nah-tee**—hour. There is no special word for "quarter" past or to in Thai. The 24-hour clock system is used in formal announcements such as on radio and television; the word **nah-li-gah** is used for "hours" and **nah-tee** for "minutes."

1:10 PM	bài mohng sìp nah-tee
1:15 PM	bài mohng sìp-hâh nah-tee
1:30 PM	bài mohng krêung
1:40 PM	èek yêe-sìp nah-tee bài sǒrng mohng
1:45 PM	èek sìp-hâh nah-tee bài sǒrng mohng
19:00	sìp-gâo nah-li-gah
20:30	yêe-sìp nah-li-gah sǎhm sìp nah-tee

THE CALENDAR

The date is expressed by the pattern:

wun ("day") + **têe** + number + month

wun têe nèung mee-nah-kom	**March 1st**
wun têe sìp-hâh may-sǎh-yon	**April 15th**

In Thailand the year is normally given according to the Buddhist Era. This is calculated by adding 543 to the AD year. So 1998 AD = 2541 (BE).

HOTELS

With tourism playing a major role in the Thai economy, it is not surprising that Bangkok offers the traveler a wide variety of accommodations, from inexpensive guesthouses to luxurious hotels. Outside Bangkok, hotels are readily found in seaside resorts, all provincial capitals, and major towns. The most luxurious facilities are found in towns geared to the international tourist trade (usually at less expensive rates than their Western counterparts), while modest yet comfortable accommodations are available throughout the kingdom for exceptionally low prices.

In the larger hotels in Bangkok and at the resorts, the staff will speak English, and some will have spent time abroad. Since using English is an important part of their job, it would be quite inappropriate for you to attempt to carry out transactions in Thai unless you are a very fluent speaker. Elsewhere, some knowledge of Thai, especially in the less-visited provinces, is both useful and appreciated.

Nearly all hotel rooms in Bangkok and the resorts are air-conditioned, but up-country an electric ceiling fan is a common alternative. All rooms will have a bathroom included, consisting of a washbasin, toilet (usually Western-style), and either a bathtub or a large water jar for Thai-style bathing.

Thais often use the English term "single room" to refer to a room with a double bed and "double room" to mean a room with two single beds, so be prepared for misunderstandings!

Meals are not usually included as part of the hotel charge; often the hotel will have its own coffee shop where both Thai and Western food are served, while international-standard hotels have their own restaurants.

"Hotel" is traditionally a rather ambiguous term in Thai. Many inexpensive "hotels" are brothels, while many slightly more respectable-looking premises are mostly used for fleeting amorous encounters. If in doubt, consult a guidebook, the Tourism Authority of Thailand, or simply ask a Thai whether it is a suitable place to stay.

USEFUL WORDS AND PHRASES

air-conditioned room	hôrng air	ห้องแอร์
air-conditioner	krêu-ung air	เครื่องแอร์
bedroom	hôrng norn	ห้องนอน
bill	bin	บิล
breakfast	ah-hăhn cháo	อาหารเช้า
coffee shop	kòrp-fêe chórp	คอฟฟี่ช้อป
double room	hôrng kôo	ห้องคู่
fan	pút lom	พัดลม
hotel	rohng-rairm	โรงแรม
key	gOOn-jair	กุญแจ
manager	pôo-jùt-gahn	ผู้จัดการ
room	hôrng	ห้อง
shower	fùk boo-a	ฝักบัว
single room	hôrng dèe-o	ห้องเดี่ยว
swimming pool	sà wâi náhm	สระว่ายน้ำ
toilet	hôrng náhm	ห้องน้ำ
twin room	hôrng kôo	ห้องคู่
window screen (*against mosquitos*)	mOOng lôo-ut	มุ้งลวด

Do you have any vacancies?
mee hôrng wâhng mái?
มีห้องว่างไหม

I have a reservation
pŏm (dee-chún) jorng hôrng wái láir-o
ผม (ดิฉัน) จองห้องไว้แล้ว

I'd like a single/double room with air-conditioning
ao hôrng dèe-o/hôrng kôo dtìt air
เอาห้องเดี่ยว / ห้องคู่ติดแอร์

What is the charge per night?
kâh hôrng wun la tâo-rài?
ค่าห้องวันละเท่าไร

I'd like a room for one night/three nights
pŏm (dee-chún) ja púk yòo keun nèung/săhm keun
ผม (ดิฉัน) จะพักอยู่คืนหนึ่ง / สามคืน

Does the room have air-conditioning?
hôrng dtìt air rĕu bplào?
ห้องติดแอร์หรือเปล่า

I don't know yet how long I'll stay
mâi sâhp wâh ja yòo nahn tâo-rài
ไม่ทราบว่าจะอยู่นานเท่าไร

May I see the room first, please?
kŏr doo hôrng gòrn dâi mái?
ขอดูห้องก่อนได้ไหม

Can you spray some mosquito repellent, please?
chôo-ay chèet yah gun yOOng hâi nòy dâi mái?
ช่วยฉีดยากันยุงให้หน่อยได้ไหม

Would you have my baggage brought up?
chôo-ay yók gra-bpăo mah hâi nòy dâi mái?
ช่วยยกกระเป๋ามาให้หน่อยได้ไหม

May I have a bottle of drinking water, please?
kŏr náhm gin kòo-ut nèung dâi mái?
ขอน้ำกินขวดหนึ่งได้ไหม

Please call me at . . . o'clock
chôo-ay rêe-uk pŏm (dee-chún) way-lah . . . mohng
ช่วยเรียกผม (ดิฉัน) เวลา ... โมง

I'll be back at . . . o'clock
pŏm (dee-chún) ja glùp way-lah . . . mohng
ผม (ดิฉัน) จะกลับเวลา ... โมง

May I leave some things in the safe?
kŏr fàhk kŏrng wái nai dtôo sáyf dâi mái?
ขอฝากของไว้ในตู้เซฟได้ไหม

My room number is . . .
pŏm (dee-chún) yòo hôrng ber . . .
ผม (ดิฉัน) อยู่ห้องเบอร์ ...

I'm leaving tomorrow
pŏm (dee-chún) ja bpai prÔOng-née
ผม (ดิฉัน) จะไปพรุ่งนี้

May I have the bill, please?
kŏr bin nòy dâi mái?
ขอบิลหน่อยได้ไหม

Can you get me a taxi?
chôo-ay rêe-uk táirk-sêe hâi nòy dâi mái?
ช่วยเรียกแท็กซี่ให้หน่อยได้ไหม

THINGS YOU'LL SEE

คอฟฟี่ช้อป	**kórp-fêe chórp**	coffee shop
ลิฟท์	**lif**	elevator
ทางออก	**tahng òrk**	exit
ชั้น	**chún**	floor

→

สอบถาม	**sòrp tăhm**	inquiries
บริการรถรับส่ง	**bor-ri-gahn rót rúp sòng**	limousine service
ชาย	**chai**	men
สุภาพบุรุษ	**sOO-pâhp bOO-ròOt**	men
ห้ามสูบบุหรี่	**hâhm sòop bOO-rèe**	no smoking
แผนกต้อนรับ	**pa-nàirk dtôrn rúp**	reception
ห้องน้ำ	**hôrng náhm**	restroom
บริการนำเที่ยว	**bor-ri-gahn num têe-o**	sightseeing tours
ยินดีต้อนรับ	**yin dee dtôrn rúp**	welcome
หญิง	**yĭng**	women
สุภาพสตรี	**sOO-pâhp sa-dtree**	women

THINGS YOU'LL HEAR

măi mee hôrng wâhng
I'm sorry, we're full

măi mee hôrng dèe-o
There are no single rooms left

măi mee hôrng kôo
There are no double rooms left

ja yòo gèe keun?
For how many nights?

chôo-ay gròrk bàirp form née nòy?
Could you fill in this form, please?

kŏr doo núng-sĕu dern tahng nòy dâi mái?
May I see your passport?

DRIVING

Bangkok's reputation as one of the world's worst traffic spots is well-deserved. With far too many cars per kilometer and a driving culture in which traffic regulations are viewed as inconveniences to be circumvented, driving in the capital itself is tiring and stressful. In theory, people drive on the left: in practice, cars tend to pass on all sides, with cheerful disregard to lane discipline and rights of way. Motorcyclists perform kamikaze stunts, cutting across and through speeding traffic with inches to spare. A further complication is that, in the ceaseless search for a solution to Bangkok's traffic problems, new restrictions—such as declaring certain routes one-way only during the rush hour—are often introduced at short notice.

Driving up-country involves different hazards. There is a good system of roads linking the provinces and a constant flow of trucks and buses carrying goods and passengers back and forth. The roads, however, are generally narrow, with little room for evasive action if the driver of an oncoming vehicle dozes off at the wheel. An often casual attitude toward the need for headlights when driving at night, both on interprovincial highways and within provincial towns, should deter the visitor from night driving except in emergencies.

If you do decide to drive in Thailand, you will need an international driver's license and nerves of steel. You will find car rental companies advertised in the local English-language newspapers. Since Thai motorists are seldom insured, parties in an accident generally negotiate—sometimes heatedly—on the spot about responsibility and payment for damage. If agreement cannot be reached amicably, the police are often called in to mediate. In any such negotiations, the foreigner is somewhat at a disadvantage.

Thailand offers an ideal climate for motorcycling, and traveling in the provinces can seem like an appealing and practical way of seeing the country. Unfortunately, many visitors, through a combination of over enthusiasm, inexperience, and poorly maintained machines, find it a costlier and more painful venture than they had originally anticipated. Unless you are an experienced rider and have sufficient mechanical know-how to judge whether the bike you are renting is in a roadworthy condition, then motorcycles are probably best left alone.

SOME COMMON ROAD SIGNS

40 ก.ม.	**sèe sìp gi-loh-mét**	40 kilometers
3 ม.	**sǎhm mét**	3 meters
4 ตัน	**sèe dtun**	4 tons
ทางโค้ง	**tahng kóhng**	bend
ระวัง	**ra-wung**	caution
อันตราย	**un-dta-rai**	danger
ทางเบี่ยง	**tahng bèe-ung**	detour
ขับช้าๆ	**kùp cháh cháh**	drive slowly
หยุด	**yòOt**	halt
หยุด—ตรวจ	**yòOt—dtròo-ut**	halt—checkpoint
โรงพยาบาล —ห้ามใช้เสียง	**rohng pa-yah-bahn —hâhm chái sěe-ung**	hospital—do not sound horn
ชิดซ้าย	**chít sái**	keep to the left
ห้ามเข้า	**hâhm kâo**	no entry
ห้ามจอด	**hâhm jòrt**	no parking
ห้ามแซง	**hâhm sairng**	no passing
ห้ามเลี้ยว	**hâhm lée-o**	no turning
ห้ามกลับรถ	**hâhm glùp rót**	no U-turns

➞

ห้ามรถทุกชนิด	**hâhm rót tÓOk cha-nít**	no vehicles
ทางรถไฟ	**tahng rót fai**	railroad
โรงเรียน	**rohng ree-un**	school

USEFUL WORDS AND PHRASES

automatic	ùt-ta-noh-mút	อัตโนมัติ
brake (*noun*)	bràyk	เบรค
breakdown	rót sěe-a	รถเสีย
car	rót	รถ
clutch	klút	คลัทช์
drive (*verb*)	kùp	ขับ
engine	krêu-ung yon	เครื่องยนต์
exhaust	tôr ai sěe-a	ท่อไอเสีย
fanbelt	sǎi pahn	สายพาน
garage (*for repairs*)	òo sǒrm rót	อู่ซ่อมรถ
gas	náhm mun	น้ำมัน
gas station	bpúm náhm mun	ปั้มน้ำมัน
gear	gee-a	เกียร์
headlights	fai nâh rót	ไฟหน้ารถ
highway	tahng dòo-un	ทางด่วน
intersection	sèe yâirk	สี่แยก
junction (*on highway*)	tahng yâirk	ทางแยก
license	bai kùp kèe	ใบขับขี่
license plate	pàirn bpâi ber rót	แผ่นป้ายเบอร์รถ
manual	gee-a meu	เกียร์มือ

mirror	gra-jòk	กระจก
motorcycle	rót mor-dter-sai	รถมอเตอร์ไซค์
road	ta-nǒn	ถนน
skid (*verb*)	cha-làirp	แฉลบ
spare parts	krêu-ung a-lài	เครื่องอะไหล่
speed (*noun*)	kwahm ray-o	ความเร็ว
speed limit	ùt-dtrah kwahm ray-o	อัตราความเร็ว
speedometer	krêu-ung wút kwahm ray-o	เครื่องวัดความเร็ว
steering wheel	poo-ung mah-lai	พวงมาลัย
taillights	fai lǔng rót	ไฟหลังรถ
tire	yahng rót	ยางรถ
tow (*verb*)	lâhk	ลาก
traffic	ja-rah-jorn	จราจร
traffic jam	rót dtìt	รถติด
traffic lights	fai sǔn-yahn ja-rah-jorn	ไฟสัญญาณจราจร
truck	rót bun-tóok	รถบรรทุก
trunk	gra-bprohng tái rót	กระโปรงท้ายรถ
van	rót dtôo	รถตู้
wheel	lór	ล้อ
windshield	gra-jòk nâh rót	กระจกหน้ารถ
windshield wipers	têe bpùt náhm fǒn	ที่ปัดน้ำฝน

I'd like some gas/oil/water
dtôrng-gahn náhm mun/náhm mun krêu-ung/náhm
ต้องการน้ำมัน / น้ำมันเครื่อง / น้ำ

Fill her up, please!
dterm náhm mun hâi dtem
เติมน้ำมันให้เต็ม

I'd like 10 liters of gas
dtôrng-gahn náhm mun sìp lít
ต้องการน้ำมันสิบลิตร

Would you check the tires, please?
chôo-ay dtròo-ut yahng hâi nòy dâi mái?
ช่วยตรวจยางให้หน่อยได้ไหม

Do you do repairs here?
têe-nêe sôrm rót dâi mái?
ที่นี่ซ่อมรถได้ไหม

Can you repair the clutch?
ja sôrm klút hâi nòy dâi mái?
จะซ่อมคลัทช์ให้หน่อยได้ไหม

How long will it take?
ja chai way-lah nahn tâo-rài?
จะใช้เวลานานเท่าไร

Where can I park?
jòrt dâi têe-nǎi?
จอดได้ที่ไหน

Can I park here?
jòrt têe-nêe dâi mái?
จอดที่นี่ได้ไหม

There is something wrong with the brakes
bràyk mâi kôy dee
เบรคไม่ค่อยดี

DIRECTIONS YOU MAY BE GIVEN

ler-ee bpai èek
straight ahead

yòo tahng sái
on the left

lée-o sái
turn left

yòo tahng kwăh
on the right

lée-o kwăh
turn right

lée-o kwăh tahng yâirk têe nèung
first on the right

lée-o sái tahng yâirk têe sŏrng
second on the left

ler-ee . . . bpai
past the . . .

The engine is overheating
krêu-ung yon rórn
เครื่องยนตร์ร้อน

I need a new tire
dtôrng-gahn yahng mài
ต้องการยางใหม่

I'd like to rent a car
yàhk ja châo rót
อยากจะเช่ารถ

Where is the nearest garage (for repairs)?
mee òo sôrm rót yòo têe-nǎi?
มีอู่ซ่อมรถอยู่ที่ไหน

How do I get to . . . ?
bpai . . . bpai tahng nǎi?
ไป ... ไปทางไหน

Is this the road to . . . ?
nêe ta-nǒn bpai . . . châi mái?
นี่ถนนไป ... ใช่ไหม

THINGS YOU'LL SEE

บริการ 24 ช.ม.	**bor-ri-gahn yêe-sìp sèe chôo-a mohng**	24-hour service
อู่	**òo**	garage
ห้ามสูบบุหรี่	**hâhm sòop bOO-rèe**	no smoking
ปะยาง	**bpà yahng**	punctures repaired
บริการซ่อมรถ	**bor-ri-gahn sôrm rót**	repair service
อะไหล่	**a-lài**	spare parts

THINGS YOU'LL HEAR

yàhk ja ao gee-a ùt-ta-noh-mút réu gee-a meu?
Would you like an automatic or a manual?

kǒr doo bai kùp kèe nòy?
May I see your license?

TRAIN TRAVEL

Traveling up-country by train in Thailand is usually slower but more comfortable than traveling by bus. The Thai railroad system consists of four major routes linking Bangkok to the north, the south, the lower northeast and the upper northeast. Three types of train operate along these routes: the slow, ordinary trains; the optimistically called "rapid" trains; and the "express" trains that are the fastest. Train reservations can be made at Bangkok's Hua Lampong Station and sleeper cars can be reserved for long-distance trips.

USEFUL WORDS AND PHRASES

baggage cart	têe lâhk gra-bpǎo	ที่ลากกระเป๋า
baggage room	têe fàhk gra-bpǎo	ที่ฝากกระเป๋า
carriage	dtôo	ตู้
connection	dtòr rót	ต่อรถ
engine	krêu-ung jùk	เครื่องจักร
first class	chún nèung	ชั้นหนึ่ง
get in	kêun	ขึ้น
get out	long	ลง
guard	pa-núk ngahn fão dtròo-ut	พนักงานเฝ้าตรวจ
lost and found	têe jâirng kŏrng hǎi	ที่แจ้งของหาย
one-way ticket	dtŏo-a bpai tahng dee-o	ตั๋วไปทางเดียว
platform	chahn chah-lah	ชานชาลา
rail	rahng rót	รางรถ
railroad	tahng rót fai	ทางรถไฟ
reservation office	têe jorng dtŏo-a	ที่จองตั๋ว

reserved seat	jorng láir-o	จองแล้ว
round-trip ticket	dtŏo-a bpai glùp	ตั๋วไปกลับ
seat	têe nûng	ที่นั่ง
second class	chún sŏrng	ชั้นสอง
sleeper car	rót norn	รถนอน
station	sa-tăhn-nee rót fai	สถานีรถไฟ
ticket	dtŏo-a	ตั๋ว
ticket office	têe jum-nài dtŏo-a	ที่จำหน่ายตั๋ว
timetable	dtah-rahng way-lah	ตารางเวลา
train	rót fai	รถไฟ
waiting room	hôrng púk	ห้องพัก
window	nâh dtàhng	หน้าต่าง

When does the train for . . . leave?
rót fai bpai . . . òrk gèe mohng?
รถไฟไป ... ออกกี่โมง

When does the train from . . . arrive?
rót fai jàhk . . . tĕung gèe mohng?
รถไฟจาก ... ถึงกี่โมง

When is the next train to . . . ?
rót fai bpai . . . ka-boo-un nâh òrk gèe mohng?
รถไฟไป ... ขบวนหน้าออกกี่โมง

When is the first train to . . . ?
rót fai bpai . . . ka-boo-un râirk òrk gèe mohng?
รถไฟไป ... ขบวนแรกออกกี่โมง

When is the last train to . . . ?
rót fai bpai . . . ka-boo-un sÒOt tái òrk gèe mohng?
รถไฟไป ... ขบวนสุดท้ายออกกี่โมง

What is the fare to . . . ?
kâh doy-ee săhn bpai . . . tâo-rài?
ค่าโดยสารไป … เท่าไร

Do I have to change?
dtôrng bplèe-un rót fai réu bplào?
ต้องเปลี่ยนรถไฟหรือเปล่า

Does the train stop at . . . ?
rót fai yÒOt têe . . . réu bplào?
รถไฟหยุดที่ … หรือเปล่า

How long does it take to get to . . . ?
bpai . . . sĕe-a way-lah nahn tâo-rài?
ไป … เสียเวลานานเท่าไร

A one-way/round-trip ticket to . . . , please
kŏr dtŏo-a bpai/bpai glùp . . .
ขอตั๋วไป / ไปกลับ …

I'd like to reserve a seat
kŏr jorng têe nûng
ขอจองที่นั่ง

Is this the right train for . . . ?
rót fai ka-boo-un née bpai . . . châi mái?
รถไฟขบวนนี้ไป … ใช่ไหม

Is this the right platform for the . . . train?
rót fai bpai . . . yòo chahn chah-lah née châi mái?
รถไฟไป … อยู่ชานชาลานี้ใช่ไหม

Which platform for the . . . train?
rót fai bpai . . . yòo chahn chah-lah năi?
รถไฟไป … อยู่ชานชาลาไหน

Could you help me with my baggage, please?
chôo-ay yók gra-bpǎo hâi nòy dâi mái?
ช่วยยกกระเป๋าให้หน่อยได้ไหม

Is this seat free?
têe nûng née wâhng réu bplào?
ที่นั่งนี้ว่างหรือเปล่า

This seat is taken
têe nûng née mâi wâhng
ที่นั่งนี้ไม่ว่าง

May I open the window?
kǒr bpèrt nâh-dtàhng nòy dâi mái?
ขอเปิดหน้าต่างหน่อยได้ไหม

May I close the window?
kǒr bpìt nâh-dtàhng nòy dâi mái?
ขอปิดหน้าต่างหน่อยได้ไหม

When do we arrive in . . . ?
těung . . . gèe mohng?
ถึง ... กี่โมง

What station is this?
têe nêe sa-tǎhn-nee a-rai?
ที่นี่สถานีอะไร

Do we stop at . . . ?
yòOt têe . . . réu bplào?
หยุดที่ ... หรือเปล่า

Would you keep an eye on my things for a moment?
chôo-ay fâo doo kǒrng hâi súk krôo dâi mái?
ช่วยเฝ้าดูของให้สักครู่ได้ไหม

THINGS YOU'LL SEE

ถึง	têung	arrivals
ที่ฝากกระเป๋า	têe fàhk gra-bpăo	baggage storage
ออก	òrk	departures
ทางเข้า	tahng kâo	entrance
ทางออก	tahng òrk	exit
เต็ม	dtem	full
สอบถาม	sòrp tăhm	information
ห้ามเข้า	hâhm kâo	no entry
ห้ามสูบบุหรี่	hâhm sòop bOO-rèe	no smoking
ชานชาลา	chahn chah-lah	platform
ประชาสัมพันธ์	bpra-chah-sŭm-pun	public relations
จองแล้ว	jorng láir-o	reserved
รถนอน	rót norn	sleeper car
รถไฟไทย	rót fai tai	Thai State Railroads
ที่จำหน่ายตั๋ว	têe jum-nài dtŏo-a	ticket office
ตารางเวลา	dtah-rahng way-lah	timetable
ว่าง	wâhng	vacant
ห้องพัก	hôrng púk	waiting room

THINGS YOU'LL HEAR

bpròht sâhp
Attention

kŏr doo dtŏo-a nòy krúp
Tickets, please

BUS AND TAXI TRAVEL

For traveling around Bangkok there is a choice of an ordinary bus, an air-conditioned bus, a **samlor** or **tuk-tuk** (a 3-wheeler motorized pedicab), and a metered taxi (avoid taking an unmetered taxi in Bangkok). There is a fixed fare on ordinary buses, but on air-conditioned buses the fare depends on distance. Bus maps are available at bookstores and hotels.

In other towns there may be some variations in the types of public transportation, such as pedal-powered or motorcycle-powered **samlors**, unmetered taxis, or various-sized pick-up trucks operating a bus-cum-taxi service.

If you plan to go by **samlor** or unmetered taxi, first check that the driver knows the location and then agree on the fare before stepping into the vehicle (the driver might ask for many times the going rate if you take the ride first). It is normal to haggle a little over the price. Tipping is not necessary.

The state-owned national bus system is inexpensive, frequent, and efficient. "Air-buses" (air-conditioned buses) operate from three major terminals in Bangkok. Refreshments are usually served en route and, on longer trips, a simple meal is provided at regular stopping points. Private companies operate more luxurious and expensive "tour bus" routes. It is usually necessary to book in advance for long-distance trips out of Bangkok—book at the relevant terminal for state-owned buses or from a central Bangkok office for private-sector buses.

USEFUL WORDS AND PHRASES

adult	pôo yài	ผู้ใหญ่
air-conditioned bus	rót air	รถแอร์
boat	reu-a	เรือ
bus	rót may	รถเมล์
bus stop	bpâi rót may	ป้ายรถเมล์

child	dèk	เด็ก
docks	tâh reu-a	ท่าเรือ
driver	kon kùp rót	คนขับรถ
fare	kâh doy-ee săhn	ค่าโดยสาร
ferry	reu-a kâhm fâhk	เรือข้ามฟาก
number 5 bus	rót may săi hâh	รถเมล์สาย ๕
passenger	pôo doy-ee săhn	ผู้โดยสาร
river	mâir náhm	แม่น้ำ
samlor	săhm-lór	สามล้อ
seat	têe nûng	ที่นั่ง
station	sa-tăhn-nee	สถานี
taxi	táirk-sêe	แท็กซี่
terminal	sa-tăhn-nee bplai tahng	สถานีปลายทาง
ticket	dtŏo-a	ตั๋ว
tour bus	rót too-a	รถทัวร์
traffic jam	rót dtìt	รถติด
tuk tuk	dtóok-dtóok	ตุ๊กๆ

Where is the bus station?
sa-tăhn-nee rót may yòo têe-năi?
สถานีรถเมล์อยู่ที่ไหน

Where is there a bus stop?
mee bpâi rót may yòo têe-năi?
มีป้ายรถเมล์อยู่ที่ไหน

Where do I get on the bus for . . . ?
bpai . . . kêun rót may têe-năi?
ไป ... ขึ้นรถเมล์ที่ไหน

What time does the bus for . . . leave?
rót bpai . . . òrk gèe mohng?
รถไป ... ออกกี่โมง

Where do I reserve a ticket for . . . ?
bpai . . . jorng dtŏo-a têe-năi?
ไป ... จองตั๋วที่ไหน

Where do I buy a ticket for . . . ?
bpai . . . séu dtŏo-a têe-năi?
ไป ... ซื้อตั๋วที่ไหน

Which buses go to . . . ?
bpai . . . ja kêun rót may săi năi?
ไป ... จะขึ้นรถเมล์สายไหน

Would you tell me when we get to . . . ?
tĕung . . . láir-o chôo-ay bòrk dôo-ay?
ถึง ... แล้วช่วยบอกด้วย

Do I have to get off yet?
dtôrng long dĕe-o née réu bplào?
ต้องลงเดี๋ยวนี้หรือเปล่า

How do you get to . . . ?
bpai . . . bpai yung-rai?
ไป ... ไปอย่างไร

Is it very far?
glai mái?
ไกลไหม

I want to go to . . .
yàhk ja bpai . . .
อยากจะไป ...

Do you go near . . . ?
bpai tăir-o . . . réu bplào?
ไปแถว ... หรือเปล่า

Could you close the window?
chôo-ay bpìt nâh-dtàhng nòy dâi mái?
ช่วยปิดหน้าต่างหน่อยได้ไหม

Could you open the window?
chôo-ay bpèrt nâh-dtàhng nòy dâi mái?
ช่วยเปิดหน้าต่างหน่อยได้ไหม

When does the last bus leave?
rót may têe-o sòòt tái òrk gèe mohng?
รถเมล์เที่ยวสุดท้ายออกกี่โมง

Do you know . . . ?
róo-jùk . . . mái?
รู้จัก ... ไหม

How much to go to . . . ?
bpai . . . tâo-rài?
ไป ... เท่าไร

That's a little expensive
pairng bpai nòy
แพงไปหน่อย

Will you go for . . . baht?
. . . bpàht bpai mái?
... บาทไปไหม

Let's settle for . . . baht
. . . bàht gôr láir-o gun
... บาทก็แล้วกัน

Turn left/right
lée-o sái/lée-o kwăh
เลี้ยวซ้าย / เลี้ยวขวา

Go straight ahead
ler-ee bpai èek
เลยไปอีก

Park over there/right here
jòrt têe-nôhn/dtrong née
จอดที่โน่น / ตรงนี้

THINGS YOU'LL SEE

รถปรับอากาศ	**rót bprùp ah-gàht**	air-conditioned bus
ถึง	**tĕung**	arrives
รับฝากของ	**rúp fàhk kŏrng**	baggage storage
ออก	**òrk**	departs
สอบถาม	**sòrp tăhm**	inquiries
ประชาสัมพันธ์	**bpra-chah-sŭm-pun**	information office
รถธรรมดา	**rót tum-ma-dah**	ordinary bus
สุขา หญิง / ชาย	**sŏO-kăh yĭng/chai**	restrooms: (women/men)
ที่จำหน่ายตั๋ว	**têe jum-nài dtŏo-a**	ticket office
กำหนดเวลาเดินรถ	**gum-nòt way-lah dern rót**	timetable
รถทัวร์	**rót too-a**	tour bus
ห้องพักผู้โดยสาร	**hôrng púk pôo-doy-ee săhn**	waiting room

RESTAURANTS

Eating out is extremely popular in Thailand, and there is a wide variety of restaurants to cater to every budget. A traditional Thai meal consists of plain boiled rice with a number of side dishes such as a curry, fried vegetables, fried meat or fish, and so on, that are shared among the diners. Some dishes are extremely hot to the Western palate, and it is perfectly reasonable to ask that the dish be made **mâi ao pèt mâhk na** ("not too hot"). Thais use a spoon and fork rather than chopsticks, and a meal is a constant "dipping in" process, where you take a small portion from the side dish and eat it with the rice. If you are taken out for a meal, you may well be invited to select one of the side dishes. If you are worried about culinary faux-pas, you can evade responsibility by saying **kOOn sùng hâi dee gwàh** ("it's better that you order for me").

If you are eating alone or are in a hurry, it is quicker to order individual dishes such as fried noodles, fried rice, noodle soup, duck-rice, and so on from one of the ubiquitous Chinese noodle shops (where you will be offered chopsticks with your noodles). Pay for the meal at the end when you are ready to leave. If you have eaten in an inexpensive noodle shop, don't leave a tip. In more expensive premises, such as coffee shops or air-conditioned or open-air restaurants, a small tip is customary. If you are taken out for a meal, don't offer to pay your share of the bill—you will probably have a chance to reciprocate as host at a later date.

USEFUL WORDS AND PHRASES

ashtray	têe-kèe-a bOO-rèe	ที่เขี่ยบุหรี่
beer	bee-a	เบียร์
bill	bin	บิล
bottle	kòo-ut	ขวด
bowl	chahm	ชาม

cake	ka-nŏm káyk	ขนมเค้ก
chef	pôr kroo-a	พ่อครัว
chopsticks	dta-gèe-up	ตะเกียบ
cigarettes	bOO-rèe	บุหรี่
coffee	gah-fair	กาแฟ
cup	tôo-ay	ถ้วย
fish sauce	náhm bplah	น้ำปลา
fork	sôrm	ส้อม
glass	gâir-o	แก้ว
knife	mêet	มีด
matches	mái kèet	ไม้ขีด
menu	may-noo	เมนู
milk	nom	นม
napkin	pâh chét meu	ผ้าเช็ดมือ
plate	jahn	จาน
receipt	bai sèt rúp ngern	ใบเสร็จรับเงิน
sandwich	sairn-wít	แซ็นวิช
snack	ah-hăhn wâhng	อาหารว่าง
soup	sóOp	ซุบ
spoon	chórn	ช้อน
sugar	náhm dtahn	น้ำตาล
table	dtó	โต๊ะ
tea	náhm chah	น้ำชา
teaspoon	chórn chah	ช้อนชา
tip	ngern típ	เงินทิบ
waiter	kon sèrp	คนเสริฟ
waitress	kon sèrp yĭng	คนเสริฟหญิง
water	náhm	น้ำ

A table for one, please
kŏr dtó sŭm-rùp kon dee-o
ขอโต๊ะสำหรับคนเดียว

A table for two, please
kŏr dtó sŭm-rùp sŏrng kon
ขอโต๊ะสำหรับสองคน

May I see the menu?
kŏr doo may-noo nòy?
ขอดูเมนูหน่อย

What would you recommend?
kOOn ja náir-num a-rai?
คุณจะแนะนำอะไร

It's better that you order for me
kOOn sùng hâi dee gwàh
คุณสั่งให้ดีกว่า

Do you have . . . ?
mee . . . mái?
มี ... ไหม

I'd like . . .
kŏr . . .
ขอ ...

Not too hot, OK?
mâi ao pèt mâhk ná
ไม่เอาเผ็ดมากนะ

Is it (very) hot?
pèt mâhk mái?
เผ็ดมากไหม

I can't eat hot food
tahn ah-hăhn pèt mâi bpen
ทานอาหารเผ็ดไม่เป็น

I can eat Thai food
tahn ah-hăhn tai bpen
ทานอาหารไทยเป็น

Could I have a glass of water, please?
kŏr náhm kăirng bplào gâir-o nèung?
ขอน้ำแข็งเปล่าแก้วหนึ่ง

Just a cup of coffee, please
kŏr gah-fair tôo-ay nèung tâo-nún
ขอกาแฟถ้วยหนึ่งเท่านั้น

Waiter/waitress!
kOOn krúp (ká)!
คุณครับ (คะ)

May we have the bill, please?
kŏr bin nòy krúp (kâ)?
ขอบิลหน่อยครับ (ค่ะ)

I didn't order this
nêe mâi dâi sùng krúp (kâ)
นี่ไม่ได้สั่งครับ (ค่ะ)

May we have some more . . . ?
kŏr . . . èek nòy dâi mái?
ขอ ... อีกหน่อยได้ไหม

That was an excellent meal, thank you
a-ròy mâhk krúp (kâ)
อร่อยมากครับ (ค่ะ)

THINGS YOU'LL HEAR

sùng láir-o réu yung krúp (ká)?
Have you ordered yet?
*(answer: **yung** = no; **sùng láir-o** = yes)*

a-ròy mái krúp (ká)?
Are you enjoying your meal, sir/madam?
*(answer: **a-ròy** = yes; **mâi a-ròy** = no)*

sùng a-rai èek mái?
Do you want to order anything else?
*(answer: **krúp (kâ)** = yes; **mâi krúp (kâ)** = no)*

tahn ah-hăhn tai/pèt bpen mái?
Can you eat Thai/hot food?
*(answer: **bpen** = yes; **mâi bpen** = no)*

THINGS YOU'LL SEE

| ร้านอาหาร | **ráhn ah-hăhn** | restaurant |
| ภัตตาคาร | **pút-dtah-kahn** | restaurant |

MENU GUIDE

APPETIZERS

อาหารว่าง	**ah-hăhn wâhng**	appetizers
ขนมจีบ	**ka-nŏm jèep**	"dim sum": pieces of meat in dough
ทอดมัน	**tôrt mun**	fish cakes
สะเต๊ะ หมู ไก่	**sa-dtáy mŏo, gài**	"satay" pork, chicken
กุ้งเผา	**gÔOng păo**	shrimps grilled over charcoal
ปอเปี้ยะทอด	**bpor bpêe-a tôrt**	spring roll

SOUPS AND CURRIES

แกงเนื้อ	**gairng néu-a**	beef curry
แกงเขียวหวานเนื้อ	**gairng kěe-o wăhn néu-a**	beef curry in a green sauce
แกงไก่	**gairng gài**	chicken curry
ต้มยำไก่	**dtôm yum gài**	chicken "tom yam"
พะแนง	**pa-nairng**	"dry" curry
แกงกะหรี่	**gairng ga-rèe**	Indian-style curry
แกงมัสหมั่น	**gairng mút-sa-mùn**	"Muslim" curry
ต้มยำกุ้ง	**dtôm yum gÔOng**	shrimp "tom yam"
แกงเผ็ด	**gairng pèt**	spicy curry
ต้มยำ	**dtôm yum**	"tom yam": a spicy soup dish
แกงส้ม	**gairng sôm**	vegetable curry (*spicy*)

| แกงจืด | **gairng jèut** | vegetable soup or stock *(mild)* |
| แกง | **gairng** | "wet" curry |

EGG DISHES

ไข่	**kài**	egg
ไข่ลวก	**kài lôo-uk**	boiled egg *(served in a glass, very soft, almost raw)*
ไข่พะโล้	**kài pa-lóh**	egg stewed in soy sauce
ไข่ดาว	**kài dao**	fried egg
ไข่เจียว	**kài jee-o**	omelette *(deep-fried)*
ไข่ยัดไส้	**kài yút sài**	omelette *(stuffed)*
ไข่ลูกเขย	**kài lôok kĕr-ee**	"son-in-law" eggs *(hard-boiled with various condiments)*

SEAFOOD

ปู	**bpoo**	crab
ปลา	**bplah**	fish
กุ้งทอดกระเทียมพริกไทย	**gÔOng tôrt gra-tee-um prík tai**	prawns fried with garlic and pepper
กุ้ง	**gÔOng**	shrimps, prawns
กุ้งผัดใบกระเพรา	**gôong pùt bai gra-prao**	shrimps fried with basil leaves
กุ้งผัดพริก	**gÔOng pùt prík**	shrimps fried with chilies
ปลาหมึก	**bplah-mèuk**	squid

ปลาหมึกผัดพริก	**bplah-mèuk pùt prík**	squid fried with chilies
ปลาหมึกทอด กระเทียมพริกไทย	**bplah-mèuk tôrt gra-tee-um prík tai**	squid fried with garlic and pepper
ปลาเปรี้ยวหวาน	**bplah bprêe-o wǎhn**	sweet and sour fish

MEAT DISHES

Beef

เนื้อ	**néu-a**	beef
เนื้อผัดน้ำมันหอย	**néu-a pùt náhm mun hǒy**	beef fried in oyster sauce
เนื้อผัดกระเทียม พริกไทย	**néu-a pùt gra-tee-um prík tai**	beef fried with garlic and pepper
เนื้อผัดขิง	**néu-a pùt kǐng**	beef fried with ginger
เนื้อสับผัดพริก กระเพรา	**néu-a sùp pùt prík gra-prao**	beef ground and fried with chilies and basil

Chicken

ไก่	**gài**	chicken
ไก่ผัดหน่อไม้	**gài pùt nòr-mái**	chicken fried with bamboo shoots
ไก่ผัดใบกระเพรา	**gài pùt bai gra-prao**	chicken fried with basil leaves
ไก่ผัดเม็ดมะม่วง หิมพานต์	**gài pùt mét ma-môo-ung hǐm-ma-pahn**	chicken fried with cashew nuts
ไก่ผัดพริก	**gài pùt prík**	chicken fried with chilies

ไก่ทอดกระเทียมพริกไทย	gài tõrt gra-tee-um prík tai	chicken fried with garlic and pepper
ไก่ผัดขิง	gài pùt kĭng	chicken fried with ginger
ไก่ย่าง	gài yâhng	chicken served roasted or barbecued

Duck

| เป็ด | bpèt | duck |
| เป็ดย่าง | bpèt yâhng | roast duck |

Pork

หมู	mŏo	pork
หมูผัดพริก	mŏo pùt prík	pork fried with chilies
หมูทอดกระเทียมพริกไทย	mŏo tõrt gra-tee-um prík tai	pork fried with garlic and pepper
หมูผัดขิง	mŏo pùt kĭng	pork fried with ginger
หมูสับผัดพริกกระเพรา	mŏo sùp pùt prík gra-prao	pork ground and fried with chilies and basil
หมูเปรี้ยวหวาน	mŏo bprêe-o wăhn	sweet and sour pork

RICE AND RICE DISHES

ข้าว	kâo	rice
ข้าวสวย	kâo sŏo-ay	boiled rice
ข้าวผัดไก่	kâo pùt gài	chicken fried rice
ข้าวมันไก่	kâo mun gài	chicken rice
ข้าวผัดปู	kâo pùt bpoo	crab fried rice

ข้าวหน้าเป็ด	**kâo nâh bpèt**	duck rice
ข้าวผัด	**kâo pùt**	fried rice
ข้าวผัดหมู	**kâo pùt mŏo**	pork fried rice
ข้าวหมูแดง	**kâo mŏo dairng**	"red" pork rice
ข้าวคลุกกะปิ	**kâo klóok ga-bpì**	rice fried with shrimp paste and served with sweet pork and shredded omelette
ข้าวต้ม	**kâo dtôm**	rice "porridge"
ข้าวผัดกุ้ง	**kâo pùt gôOng**	shrimp fried rice
ข้าวเหนียว	**kâo nĕe-o**	"sticky" rice

NOODLES AND NOODLE DISHES

หมี่กรอบ	**mèe gròrp**	crispy noodles
ก๋วยเตี๋ยวแห้ง	**gŏo-ay dtĕe-o hâirng**	"dry" noodles (without soup)
บะหมี่	**ba-mèe**	egg noodles
ผัดซีอิ๊ว	**pùt see éw**	noodles fried in soy sauce
ผัดราดหน้า	**pùt râht nâh**	noodles served with fried meat and vegetables in a thick gravy
ก๋วยเตี๋ยวน้ำ	**gŏo-ay dtĕe-o náhm**	noodle soup
ก๋วยเตี๋ยว	**gŏo-ay dtĕe-o**	rice-flour noodles
ผัดไทย	**pùt tai**	Thai-style fried noodles
ขนมจีน	**ka-nŏm jeen**	Thai vermicelli

VEGETABLES

หน่อไม้	**nòr mái**	bamboo shoots
ถั่วงอก	**tòo-a ngôrk**	bean sprouts
ถั่วฝักยาว	**tòo-a fùk yao**	black-eyed peas
กระหล่ำปลี	**gra-lùm-bplee**	cabbage
พริก	**prík**	chili
ข้าวโพด	**kâo pôht**	corn
แตงกวา	**dtairng-gwah**	cucumber
กระเทียม	**gra-tee-um**	garlic
ขิง	**kǐng**	ginger
พริกหยวก	**prík yòo-uk**	green pepper
ผักบุ้ง	**pùk bÔOng**	morning glory
เห็ด	**hèt**	mushroom
หัวหอม	**hǒo-a hǒrm**	onion
ต้นหอม	**dtôn hǒrm**	scallion
ถั่วลันเตา	**tòo-a lun-dtao**	snow pea
ผักคะน้า	**pùk ka-náh**	spring greens
มะเขือเทศ	**ma-kěu-a tâyt**	tomato
ผัก	**pùk**	vegetable

FRUIT

กล้วย	**glôo-ay**	banana
มะพร้าว	**ma-práo**	coconut
น้อยหน่า	**nóy-nàh**	custard apple
ทุเรียน	**tOO-ree-un**	durian
ผลไม้	**pǒn-la-mái**	fruit
ส้มโอ	**sôm oh**	grapefruit

ฝรั่ง	**fa-rùng**	guava
ขนุน	**ka-nŏOn**	jackfruit
ลำใย	**lum-yai**	longan
ลิ้นจี่	**lín-jèe**	lychee
มะม่วง	**ma-môo-ung**	mango
ส้ม	**sôm**	orange
มะละกอ	**ma-la-gor**	papaya
สับปะรด	**sùp-bpa-rót**	pineapple
เงาะ	**ngór**	rambutan
ชมพู่	**chom-pôo**	rose apple
ละมุด	**la-mÓOt**	sapodilla
แตงโม	**dtairng moh**	watermelon

BASIC CONDIMENTS AND METHODS OF COOKING

ต้ม	**dtôm**	boiled
ย่าง	**yâhng**	charcoal-grilled
น้ำพริก	**náhm prík**	chili paste
น้ำปลา	**náhm bplah**	fish sauce
ทอด	**tôrt**	fried, deep-fried
ผัด	**pùt**	fried, stir-fried
อบ	**òp**	oven-cooked
พริกไทย	**prík tai**	pepper
น้ำซีอิ๊ว	**náhm see éw**	soy sauce
ปิ้ง	**bpîng**	toasted
น้ำส้ม	**náhm sôm**	vinegar

DRINKS

เบียร์	**bee-a**	beer
น้ำโซดา	**náhm soh-dah**	carbonated water
โคล่า	**koh-lâh**	Coca Cola®
น้ำมะพร้าว	**náhm ma-práo**	coconut juice
กาแฟ	**gah-fair**	coffee
โอเลี้ยง	**oh-lée-ung**	coffee served black, iced, and with lots of sugar
เครื่องดื่ม	**krêu-ung dèum**	drink(s)
น้ำผลไม้	**náhm pŏn-la-mái**	fruit juice
น้ำแข็ง	**náhm kăirng**	ice
น้ำมะนาว	**náhm ma-nao**	lime juice
แม่โขง	**mâir-kŏhng**	Mekhong Whiskey®
น้ำส้ม	**náhm sôm**	orange juice *(bottled)*
น้ำส้มคั้น	**náhm sôm kún**	orange juice *(fresh)*
เป๊ปซี่	**bpép-sêe**	Pepsi Cola®
น้ำโปลาริส	**náhm bpoh-la-rít**	Polaris water® *(bottled drinking water)*
น้ำชา	**náhm chah**	tea
น้ำ	**náhm**	water
น้ำแข็งเปล่า	**náhm kăirng bplào**	water – a glass of water with ice

SHOPPING

Thailand offers the visitor an assortment of shopping facilities ranging from traditional markets to ultra-modern multistory shopping plazas. Stores vary in their opening times, but many stay open until 7 or 8 PM during the week and remain open on Sundays. While bargaining is inappropriate in most stores, it is an essential part of shopping in markets and at sidewalk stalls. Ideally, you should try to get some idea of what a reasonable price is before attempting to bargain. Then, negotiations should be carried out in a good-humored manner.

USEFUL WORDS AND PHRASES

bookstore	ráhn kǎi núng-sěu	ร้านขายหนังสือ
buy	séu	ซื้อ
cash register	têe chum-rá ngern	ที่ชำระเงิน
department store	hâhng	ห้าง
drugstore	ráhn kǎi yah	ร้านขายยา
fashion	fair-chûn	แฟชั่น
gold	torng	ทอง
hill-tribe handicrafts	hùt-ta-gum chao kǎo	หัตถกรรมชาวเขา
inexpensive	tòok	ถูก
ladies' wear	sêu-pâh sa-dtree	เสื้อผ้าสตรี
market	dta-làht	ตลาด
menswear	sêu-pâh bOO-ròOt	เสื้อผ้าบุรุษ
newsstand	ráhn kǎi núng-sěu pim	ร้านขายหนังสือพิมพ์
price	rah-kah	ราคา
receipt	bai sèt rúp ngern	ใบเสร็จรับเงิน

sale	lót rah-kah	ลดราคา
shoe store	ráhn kǎi rorng táo	ร้านขายรองเท้า
go shopping	bpai séu kǒrng	ไปซื้อของ
silverware	krêu-ung ngern	เครื่องเงิน
special offer	lót pi-sàyt	ลดพิเศษ
spend	sěe-a ngern	เสียเงิน
stationery store	ráhn kǎi krêu-ung kěe-un	ร้านขายเครื่องเขียน
store	ráhn	ร้าน
supermarket	sóop-bpêr-mah-gêt	ซุปเปอร์มาร์เก็ต
tailor	ráhn dtùt sêu-a	ร้านตัดเสื้อ
Thai silk	pâh-mǎi tai	ผ้าไหมไทย
travel agent	bor-ri-sùt num têe-o	บริษัทนำเที่ยว

I'd like . . .
dtôrng-gahn . . .
ต้องการ ...

Do you have . . . ?
mee . . . mái?
มี ... ไหม

How much is this?
nêe tâo-rài?
นี่เท่าไร

Where is the . . . department?
pa-nàirk kǎi . . . yòo têe-nǎi?
แผนกขาย ... อยู่ที่ไหน

Do you have any more of these?
yàhng née mee èek mái?
อย่างนี้มีอีกไหม

I'd like to change this, please
kŏr bplèe-un un née nòy dâi mái?
ขอเปลี่ยนอันนี้หน่อยได้ไหม

Do you have anything less expensive?
tòok gwàh née mee mái?
ถูกกว่านี้มีไหม

Do you have anything larger?
yài gwàh née mee mái?
ใหญ่กว่านี้มีไหม

Do you have anything smaller?
lék gwàh née mee mái?
เล็กกว่านี้มีไหม

Does it come in other colors?
mee sĕe èun èek mái?
มีสีอื่นอีกไหม

Could you wrap it for me?
chôo-ay hòr hâi nòy dâi mái?
ช่วยห่อให้หน่อยได้ไหม

May I have a receipt?
kŏr bai sèt rúp ngern
ขอใบเสร็จรับเงิน

Can I try it (them) on?
kŏr lorng sài doo dâi mái?
ขอลองใส่ดูได้ไหม

Where do I pay?
jài ngern têe-năi?
จ่ายเงินที่ไหน

Can I have a refund?
kŏr ngern keun hâi dâi mái?
ขอเงินคืนให้ได้ไหม

I'm just looking
chom doo tâo-nún
ชมดูเท่านั้น

I'll come back later
dĕe-o ja glùp mah mài
เดี๋ยวจะกลับมาใหม่

That's a bit expensive
pairng bpai nòy krúp (kâ)
แพงไปหน่อยครับ (ค่ะ)

Could you lower the price a little?
lót rah-kah nòy dâi mái?
ลดราคาหน่อยได้ไหม

How about . . . baht?
. . . bàht dâi mái?
... บาทได้ไหม

THINGS YOU'LL SEE

บาท	**bàht**	baht (unit of currency)
ปิด	**bpìt**	closed
ใบละ ...	**bai la . . .**	. . . each
ชั้น	**chún**	floor
เปิด	**bpèrt**	open
โหลละ ...	**lŏh la . . .**	. . . per dozen
กิโลละ ...	**gi-loh la . . .**	. . . per kilogram
ราคา	**rah-kah**	price
ลดราคา	**lót rah-kah**	sale
ลดพิเศษ	**lót pi-sàyt**	special reduction

THINGS YOU'LL HEAR

rúp a-rai krúp (ká)?
Are you being helped?

mee sàyt sa-dtahng mái krúp (ká)?
Do you have anything smaller? (money)

dtorn née kăi mòt krúp (kâ)
I'm sorry, we're out of stock

mee tâo née la krúp (kâ)
This is all we have

séu a-rai èek mái krúp (ká)?
Will there be anything else?

AT THE HAIRDRESSER'S

Appearance is very important in Thailand, and hairdressers and barbers catering to a range of income levels are plentiful. The most sophisticated salons in Bangkok are similar to those in the West. Even modest places often offer a full range of beauty care and may also double as dressmakers. It is generally not necessary to make an appointment.

USEFUL WORDS AND PHRASES

appointment	nút	นัด
bangs	pŏm máh	ผมม้า
beard	krao	เครา
blond	pŏm sĕe torng	ผมสีทอง
blow-dry	bpào hâi hâirng	เป่าให้แห้ง
brush	bprairng pŏm	แปรงผม
comb	wĕe	หวี
conditioner	kreem nôo-ut pŏm	ครีมนวดผม
curlers	krêu-ung dùt pŏm	เครื่องตัดผม
curling iron	keem dùt pŏm	คีมดัดผม
curly	pŏm yìk	ผมหยิก
dark	dum	ดำ
gel	kreem sài pŏm	ครีมใส่ผม
hair	pŏm	ผม
haircut	dtùt pŏm	ตัดผม
hairdresser	chûng dtùt pŏm	ช่างตัดผม
hairdresser's	ráhn dtùt pŏm	ร้านตัดผม
hair dryer	krêu-ung bpào pŏm	เครื่องเป่าผม
long	yao	ยาว
moustache	nòo-ut	หนวด

part	sàirk	แสก
perm	dùt pŏm	ดัดผม
shampoo	yah sà pom	ยาสระผม
shave	gohn	โกน
shaving cream	kreem gohn nòo-ut	ครีมโกนหนวด
short	sûn	สั้น
styling mousse	kreem dtàirng pŏm	ครีมแต่งผม
wash and set	sà sét	สระเซ็ท
wavy	bpen lorn	เป็นลอน

I'd like to make an appointment
yàhk nút way-lah tum pŏm
อยากนัดเวลาทำผม

Just a trim, please
dtùt nít-nòy tâo-nún
ตัดนิดหน่อยเท่านั้น

Not too much off
mâi dtùt òrk mâhk
ไม่ตัดออกมาก

A bit more off here, please
dtùt dtrong née òrk èek nòy
ตัดตรงนี้ออกอีกหน่อย

I'd like a cut and blow-dry
yàhk ja dtùt láir bpào hâi hâirng
อยากจะตัดและเป่าให้แห้ง

I'd like a perm
yàhk ja dùt pŏm
อยากจะดัดผม

THINGS YOU'LL SEE

บาร์เบอร์	**bah-ber**	barber
เสริมสวย	**sěrm sǒo-ay**	beauty care
ตัดเสื้อ	**dtùt sêu-a**	dressmaker
แต่งหน้า	**dtàirng nâh**	facial
นวดหน้า	**nôo-ut nâh**	facial massage
ตัดผม	**dtùt pǒm**	haircut
ดัดผม	**dùt pǒm**	hair styling
ทำเล็บ	**tum lép**	manicure
เซ็ทผม	**sét pǒm**	set
โกนหนวด	**gohn nòo-ut**	shave
สระ	**sà**	wash

THINGS YOU'LL HEAR

yàhk ja tum bàirp nǎi?
How would you like it?

kâir née sûn por réu yung?
Is that short enough?

ja sài kreem nôo-ut pǒm mái?
Would you like any conditioner?

POST OFFICES AND BANKS

Thailand has a relatively efficient postal system, but use a
courier if you want to mail valuables. Generally, post offices
are open from 8:30 AM to 4:30 PM on weekdays and 9 AM to
noon on Saturdays. Bangkok's Central Post Office on New Road
and large branches in major towns, however, stay open until
8 PM on weekdays and may also open on Sunday mornings.
In addition to normal post office services, they may offer a
parcel-packing service and 24-hour telegram service. Stamps
can also be purchased from and letters mailed at major hotels.

Banks are open from 8:30 AM to 3:30 PM on weekdays. Many
banks in Bangkok have currency exchange kiosks outside the
main building. These are often open until 8 or 9 PM every day.
Currency exchange facilities are also available at Bangkok's
Don Muang airport (24-hour service) and major hotels.

Thailand's unit of currency is the **baht** (**B**), which is made up
of 100 **satang**. Banknotes come in 10, 20, 50, 100, 500, and
1,000 **baht** denominations; coins come in 25 and 50 **satang**
and 1, 5, and 10 **baht** demoninations.

USEFUL WORDS AND PHRASES

aerogram	jòt-mǎi ah-gàht	จดหมายอากาศ
airmail	tahng ah-gàht	ทางอากาศ
baht (*currency*)	bàht	บาท
bank	ta-nah-kahn	ธนาคาร
bill (*money*)	ton-na-bùt, báirnk	ธนบัตร; แบ็งค์
change (*verb*)	lâirk bplèe-un	แลกเปลี่ยน
check	chék	เช็ค
collection	gèp jòt-mǎi jàhk dtôo	เก็บจดหมายจากตู้
counter	kao-dtêr	เคาน์เตอร์

68

customs form	form sĕe-a pah-sĕe	ฟอร์มเสียภาษี
delivery	sòng jòt-măi dtahm bâhn	ส่งจดหมายตามบ้าน
deposit (*verb*)	fàhk ngern	ฝากเงิน
dollar (US)	ngern a-may-ri-gun don-lah	เงินอเมริกันดอลลาร์
exchange rate	ùt-dtrah lâirk bplèe-un	อัตราแลกเปลี่ยน
form	bàirp form	แบบฟอร์ม
letter	jòt-măi	จดหมาย
mail (*noun*)	jòt-măi	จดหมาย
mailbox	dtôo bprai-sa-nee	ตู้ไปรษณีย์
mailman	bOO-ròOt bprai-sa-nee	บุรุษไปรษณีย์
money order	ta-nah-nút	ธนาณัติ
package	hòr	ห่อ
post (*verb*)	sòng jòt-măi	ส่งจดหมาย
postage rates	ùt-dtrah kâh bprai-sa-nee	อัตราค่าไปรษณีย์
postal code	ra-hùt bprai-sa-nee	รหัสไปรษณีย์
postal order	chék-bprai-sa-nee	เช็คไปรษณีย์
postcard	póht-gáht	โปสการ์ด
poste restante	poste restante	โพชทเร็ชทานท์
post office	bprai-sa-nee	ไปรษณีย์
registered letter	jòt-măi long ta-bee-un	จดหมายลงทะเบียน
satang (*currency*)	sa-dtahng	สตางค์
stamp	sa-dtairm	แสตมป์
surface mail	sòng tahng reu-a	ส่งทางเรือ

telegram	toh-ra-lâyk	โทรเลข
traveler's check	chék dern tahng	เช็คเดินทาง
zip code	ra-hùt bprai-sa-nee	รหัสไปรษณีย์

How much is a letter/postcard to . . . ?
sòng jòt-măi/póht-gáht bpai . . . tâo-rài?
ส่งจดหมาย / โปสการ์ดไป ... เท่าไร

I would like three 9-baht stamps
kŏr sa-dtairm gâo bàht săhm doo-ung
ขอแสตมป์เก้าบาทสามดวง

I want to register this letter
yàhk ja long ta-bee-un-jòt-măi née
อยากจะลงทะเบียนจดหมายนี้

I want to send this package to . . .
yàhk ja sòng hòr née bpai . . .
อยากจะส่งห่อนี้ไป ...

How long does mail to . . . take?
sòng bpai . . . chái way-lah nahn tâo-rài?
ส่งไป ... ใช้เวลานานเท่าไร

Where can I mail this?
nêe sòng dâi têe-năi?
นี่ส่งได้ที่ไหน

Is there any mail for me?
mee jòt-măi sŭm-rùp pŏm (dee-chún) mái?
มีจดหมายสำหรับผม (ดิฉัน) ไหม

I'd like to send a telegram to . . .
dtōrng-gahn sòng toh-ra-lâyk bpai . . .
ต้องการส่งโทรเลขไป ...

This is to go airmail
nêe sòng bpai tahng ah-gàht
นี่ส่งไปทางอากาศ

I'd like to change this into . . .
kŏr lâirk nêe bpen . . .
ขอแลกนี่เป็น ...

Can I cash these traveler's checks?
kŏr lâirk chék dern tahng dâi mái?
ขอแลกเช็คเดินทางได้ไหม

What is the exchange rate for the dollar?
ùt-dtrah lâirk bplèe-un ngern a-may-ri-gun don-lah tâo-rài?
อัตราแลกเปลี่ยนเงินอเมริกันดอลลาร์เท่าไร

ที่อยู่	**têe yòo**	address
ทางอากาศ	**tahng ah-gàht**	airmail
กรุงเทพ ฯ	**grOOng-tâyp**	Bangkok
ธนาคาร	**ta-nah-kahn**	bank
ฝากเงิน	**fàhk ngern**	deposits

อัตราแลกเปลี่ยน
  เงินตราต่างประเทศ
	**ùt-dtrah lâirk
	  bplèe-un ngern
	  dtrah dtàhng
	  bpra-tâyt**
		exchange rate

ด่วน	**dòo-un**	express
กรอก	**gròrk**	fill in (form, etc.)

แลกเปลี่ยนเงินตรา
  ต่างประเทศ
	**lâirk bplèe-un
	  ngern dtrah
	  dtàhng bpra-tâyt**
		foreign exchange

→

สอบถาม	**sòrp tăhm**	inquiries
จดหมาย	**jòt-măi**	letters
ตู้ไปรษณีย์	**dtôo bprai-sa-nee**	mailbox
เวลาปิด-เปิด	**way-lah bpìt – bpèrt**	opening hours
ที่อื่น	**têe èun**	other places
พัสดุ	**pú-sa-dÒO**	packages (counter)
ไปรษณีย์	**bprai-sa-nee**	post office
ที่ทำการไปรษณีย์	**têe tum gahn bprai-sa-nee**	post office
ลงทะเบียน	**long ta-bee-un**	registered mail
ผู้ส่ง	**pôo sòng**	sender
ไปรษณียากร	**bprai-sa-nee-ya-gorn**	stamps
โทรเลข	**toh-rah-lâyk**	telegrams
ถอนเงิน	**tŏrn ngern**	withdrawals

THINGS YOU'LL HEAR

gròrk bàirp form née
Fill in this form

kŏr doo núng-sĕu dern tahng nòy dâi mái?
Could I see your passport, please?

sòng bpai tahng ah-gàht réu tahng reu-a?
Do you want to send it by air or surface mail?

TELEPHONES

Most public phone booths are for domestic calls only. Buy a phonecard from a grocery store or post office if you want to make a long-distance, domestic call. To make an international call, look for one of the yellow public phones at airports and in busy tourist areas, or call direct or via the operator from your hotel. Some major post offices, such as the Central Post Office on New Road in Bangkok, have a separate annex for international phone calls.

USEFUL WORDS AND PHRASES

call (*verb*)	toh-ra-sùp	โทรศัพท์
code	ra-hùt toh-ra-sùp	รหัสโทรศัพท์
collect call	toh-ra-sùp gèp ngern bplai tahng	โทรศัพท์เก็บเงินปลายทาง
dial (*verb*)	mŏOn ber	หมุนเบอร์
extension	dtòr	ต่อ
international call	toh-ra-sùp dtàhng bpra-tâyt	โทรศัพท์ต่างประเทศ
number	ber toh-ra-sùp	เบอร์โทรศัพท์
operator	pa-núk ngahn toh-ra sùp	พนักงานโทรศัพท์
receiver	hŏo toh-ra-sùp	หูโทรศัพท์
telephone	toh-ra-sùp	โทรศัพท์
telephone booth	dtôo toh-ra-sùp	ตู้โทรศัพท์
telephone directory	sa-mòot măi-lâyk toh-ra-sùp	สมุดหมายเลขโทรศัพท์
wrong number	toh pìt	โทรผิด

Where is the nearest phone booth?
tăir-o née mee dtōo toh-ra-sùp yòo têe-năi?
แถวนี้มีตู้โทรศัพท์อยู่ที่ไหน

Is there a telephone directory?
mee sa-mòot măi-lâyk toh-ra-sùp mái?
มีสมุดหมายเลขโทรศัพท์ไหม

Can I call abroad from here?
ja toh-ra-sùp bpai dtàhng bpra-tâyt jàhk têe nêe dâi mái?
จะโทรศัพท์ไปต่างประเทศจากที่นี่ได้ไหม

How much is a call to . . . ?
toh-ra-sùp bpai . . . tâo-rài?
โทรศัพท์ไป ... เท่าไร

I would like to make a collect call
kŏr hâi gèp ngern bplai tahng
ขอให้เก็บเงินปลายทาง

I would like a number in . . .
dtôrng-gahn dtòr ber toh-ra-sùp têe . . .
ต้องการต่อเบอร์โทรศัพท์ที่ ...

Hello, this is . . . speaking
"hello", pŏm (dee-chún) . . . pôot krúp (kâ)
ฮัลโหล ผม (ดิฉัน) ... พูดครับ (ค่ะ)

Is that . . . ?
têe-nôhn . . . châi mái?
ที่โน่น ... ใช่ไหม

Speaking
gum-lung pôot krúp (kâ)
กำลังพูดครับ (ค่ะ)

I would like to speak to . . .
kŏr pôot gùp . . . nòy, dâi mái?
ขอพูดกับ ... หน่อยได้ไหม

Extension . . . , please
kŏr dtòr ber . . .
ขอต่อเบอร์ ...

Please tell him . . . called
chôo-ay bòrk káo wâh mee . . . toh mah
ช่วยบอกเขาว่ามี ... โทรมา

Could you ask him to call me back, please?
chôo-ay bòrk hâi káo toh mah mài
ช่วยบอกให้เขาโทรมาใหม่

My number is . . .
ber toh-ra-sùp pŏm (dee-chún) . . .
เบอร์โทรศัพท์ผม (ดิฉัน) ...

Do you know where he is?
sâhp mái wâh káo yòo têe-năi?
ทราบไหมว่าเขาอยู่ที่ไหน

When will he be back?
káo ja glùp mah mêu-rai?
เขาจะกลับมาเมื่อไร

Could I leave him a message?
kŏr fàhk sùng a-rai nòy dâi mái?
ขอฝากสั่งอะไรหน่อยได้ไหม

I'll call back later
dĕe-o ja toh mah mài
เดี๋ยวจะโทรมาใหม่

Sorry, wrong number
kŏr-tôht toh pìt ber
ขอโทษโทรผิดเบอร์

THINGS YOU'LL SEE

บาท	**bàht**	baht (unit of currency)
รหัส	**ra-hùt**	code
เหรียญ	**rĕe-un**	coin
ต่อ	**dtòr**	extension
ต่างประเทศ	**dtàhng bpra-tâyt**	international
โทรศัพท์ต่างประเทศ	**toh-ra-sùp dtàhng bpra-tâyt**	international call(s)
โทรศัพท์ทางไกล	**toh-ra-sùp tahng glai**	long-distance call(s)
เสีย	**sĕe-a**	out of order
ตู้โทรศัพท์สาธารณะ	**dtôo toh-ra-sùp săh-tah-ra-ná**	public telephone booth
โทรศัพท์	**toh-ra-sùp**	telephone

THINGS YOU'LL HEAR

ja pôot gùp krai krúp (ká)?
Whom would you like to speak to?

kOOn toh ber pìt
You've got the wrong number

krai pôot krúp (ká)?
Who's speaking?

ber toh-ra-sùp kOOn a-rai krúp (ká)?
What is your number?

pôot dung dung nòy dâi mái?
Could you speak louder, please?

káo mâi yòo krúp (kâ)
Sorry, he's not in

káo ja glùp . . . mohng
He'll be back at . . . o'clock

chôo-ay toh mah mài prÔOng-née krúp (ká)
Please call again tomorrow

ja bòrk káo wâh kOOn toh mah
I'll tell him you called

mee a-rai ja sùng mái?
Do you want to leave a message?

dtòr ber a-rai krúp (ká)?
What extension number do you want?

săi mâi wâhng
The line's busy

HEALTH

In the event of serious injury or illness, medical expenses can prove costly, so medical insurance is essential. Appointments to see a doctor at a private hospital or clinic can be made on short notice. All doctors will speak English, and many have had a number of years of advanced training or practice in the US. Thai doctors are sometimes rather liberal in the types and quantities of medicines they prescribe, even for relatively minor illnesses. If you are unhappy about the prescription, discuss it with the doctor. For less serious problems, it is possible to seek advice and purchase the appropriate medicines from a pharmacy without a prescription.

USEFUL WORDS AND PHRASES

accident	OO-bùt-dti-hàyt	อุบัติเหตุ
acupuncture	fŭng kěm	ฝังเข็ม
ambulance	rót pa-yah-bahn	รถพยาบาล
anemic	loh-hìt jahng	โลหิตจาง
appendicitis	rôhk sâi dtìng	โรคไส้ติ่ง
appendix	sâi dtìng	ไส้ติ่ง
aspirin	air-sa-bprin	แอสไพริน
asthma	rôhk hèut	โรคหืด
backache	bpòo-ut lŭng	ปวดหลัง
bandage	pâh pun plăir	ผ้าพันแผล
(*adhesive*)	bpláh-sa-dtêr	ปลาสเตอร์
bite (*by dog*)	măh gùt	หมากัด
(*by insect*)	ma-lairng gùt	แมลงกัด
bladder	gra-pór bpù-săh-wá	กระเพาะปัสสาวะ
blister	plăir porng	แผลพอง
blood	lêu-ut	เลือด

blood donor	pôo bor-ri-jàhk lêu-ut	ผู้บริจาคเลือด
burn (*noun*)	mâi	ไหม้
cancer	ma-reng	มะเร็ง
chest	nâh-òk	หน้าอก
chicken pox	ee-sòOk ee-săi	อีสุกอีใส
cholera	a-hi-wah	อหิวาต์
cold (*noun*)	bpen wùt	เป็นหวัด
concussion	sa-mŏrng tòok gra-tóp gra-teu-un	สมองถูกกระทบกระเทือน
constipation	tórng pòok	ท้องผูก
contact lenses	korn-táirk layn	คอนแท็คท์เลนส์
corn	dtah bplah	ตาปลา
cough (*noun*)	ai	ไอ
cut (*noun*)	roy bàht	รอยบาด
dentist	mŏr fun	หมอฟัน
diabetes	rôhk bao wăhn	โรคเบาหวาน
diarrhea	tórng sĕe-a	ท้องเสีย
dizzy	wee-un hŏo-a	เวียนหัว
doctor	mŏr	หมอ
drugstore	ráhn kăi yah	ร้านขายยา
dysentery	rôhk bìt	โรคบิด
earache	bpòo-ut hŏo	ปวดหู
fever	kâi	ไข้
filling	òOt fun	อุดฟัน
first aid	gahn bpa-tŏm pa-yah-bahn	การปฐมพยาบาล
flu	kâi wùt	ไข้หวัด
fracture	gra-dòok hùk	กระดูกหัก

German measles	rôhk hùt yer-ra-mun	โรคหัดเยอรมัน
glasses	wâirn dtah	แว่นตา
hay fever	kâi-jahm	ไข้จาม
headache	bpòo-ut hŏo-a	ปวดหัว
heart	hŏo-a jai	หัวใจ
heart attack	hŏo-a jai wai	หัวใจวาย
hemorrhage	dtòk lêu-ut	ตกเลือด
hepatitis	dtùp ùk-sàyp	ตับอักเสบ
hospital	rohng pa-yah-bahn	โรงพยาบาล
ill	mâi sa-bai	ไม่สบาย
injection	chèet yah	ฉีดยา
itch	kun	คัน
jaundice	rôhk dee-sāhn	โรคดีซ่าน
kidney	tai	ไต
lump	néu-a ngôrk	เนื้องอก
malaria	mah-lay-ree-a	มาเลเรีย
massage	nôo-ut	นวด
measles	rôhk hut	โรคหัด
migraine	bpòo-ut hŏo-a kâhng dee-o	ปวดหัวข้างเดียว
motion sickness (*air*)	mao krêu-ung bin	เมาเครื่องบิน
(*car*)	mao rót	เมารถ
(*sea*)	mao reu-a	เมาเรือ
mumps	kahng toom	คางทูม
nausea	ah-gahn klêun hĕe-un	อาการคลื่นเทียน
nurse	nahng pa-yah-bahn	นางพยาบาล
operation	gahn pàh dtùt	การผ่าตัด

optician	jùk-sŎO pâirt	จักษุแพทย์
pain	kwahm jèp bpòo-ut	ความเจ็บปวด
penicillin	yah pen-ní-seen-lin	ยาเพนนิซีลลิน
pneumonia	bpòrt ùk-sàyp	ปอดอักเสบ
pregnant	mee tórng	มีท้อง
prescription	bai sùng yah	ใบสั่งยา
prickly heat	pòt	ผด
rheumatism	rôhk bpòo-ut nai kôr	โรคปวดในข้อ
scald (noun)	tòok náhm rórn lôo-uk	ถูกน้ำร้อนลวก
scratch (noun)	roy kòo-un	รอยข่วน
smallpox	kâi tor-ra-pít	ไข้ทรพิษ
sore throat	jèp kor	เจ็บคอ
splint	fèu-uk	เฝือก
splinter	sa-gèt mái	สะเก็ดไม้
sprain	klét	เคล็ด
sting (verb: insect)	dtòy	ต่อย
stomach	tórng	ท้อง
stomachache	bpòo-ut tórng	ปวดท้อง
temperature	bpen kâi	เป็นไข้
tonsils	dtòrm torn-sin	ต่อมทอนซิล
toothache	bpòo-ut fun	ปวดฟัน
traditional doctor (herbalist)	mŏr păirn boh-rahn	หมอแผนโบราณ
traditional medicine	yah păirn boh-rahn	ยาแผนโบราณ
ulcer	plăir gra-pór	แผลกระเพาะ
vaccination	chèet wúk-seen	ฉีดวัคซีน
vomit (verb)	ah-jee-un	อาเจียน
whooping cough	ai gron	ไอกรน

I have a pain in . . .
jèp têe . . .
เจ็บที่ ...

I do not feel well
róo-sèuk mâi sa-bai
รู้สึกไม่สบาย

I feel faint
róo-sèuk ja bpen lom
รู้สึกจะเป็นลม

I feel sick
róo-sèuk ja ah-jee-un
รู้สึกจะอาเจียน

I feel dizzy
róo-sèuk wee-un hŏo-a
รู้สึกเวียนหัว

It hurts here
jèp dtrong née
เจ็บตรงนี้

It's a sharp pain
jèp bpòo-ut yàhng rairng
เจ็บปวดอย่างแรง

It hurts all the time
jèp dta-lòrt way-lah
เจ็บตลอดเวลา

It only hurts now and then
jèp bpen bahng krúng bahng krao
เจ็บเป็นบางครั้งบางคราว

It stings
sàirp
แสบ

It aches
bpòo-ut
ปวด

I have a temperature
bpen kâi
เป็นไข้

I normally take . . .
bpòk-ka-dtì gin yah . . .
ปกติกินยา ...

I'm allergic to . . .
pŏm (dee-chún) páir . . .
ผม (ดิฉัน) แพ้ ...

Have you got anything for . . . ?
mee yah gâir . . . mái?
มียาแก้ ... ไหม

I need a new filling
dtôrng òot fun mài
ต้องอุดฟันใหม่

THINGS YOU'LL SEE

รถพยาบาล	**rót pa-yah bahn**	ambulance
คลีนิค	**klee-nìk**	clinic
ทันตแพทย์	**tun-dta-pâirt**	dentist
ทำฟัน	**tum fun**	dentist's office

→

นายแพทย์ (น.พ.)	**nai pâirt**	doctor (male)
แพทย์หญิง (พ.ญ.)	**pâirt yĭng**	doctor (female)
ตรวจสายตา	**dtròo-ut săi-dtah**	eye test
โรงพยาบาล	**rohng pa-yah-bahn**	hospital
ฉีดยา	**chèet yah**	injection
ยา	**yah**	medicine
ใบสั่งยา	**bai sùng yah**	prescription
เอ็กซเรย์	**"X-ray"**	X-ray

THINGS YOU'LL HEAR

rúp-bpra-tahn krúng la . . . mét
Take . . . pills/tablets at a time

dèum náhm bpai dôo-ay
With water

wun la krúng/sŏrng krúng/săhm krúng
Once/twice/three times a day

way-lah kâo norn tâo-nún
Only when you go to bed

bpòk-ka-dti rúp-bpra-tahn a-rai?
What do you normally take?

kít wâh koo-un bpai hăh mŏr
I think you should see a doctor

mâi mee krúp (kâ)
I'm sorry, we don't have that

dtôrng mee bai sùng yah
For that you need a prescription

MINI-DICTIONARY

a *no articles in Thai*
absorbent cotton sŭm-lee   สำลี
accident OO-bùt-dti-hàyt   อุบัติเหตุ
adaptor krêu-ung bplairng fai fáh   เครื่องแปลงไฟฟ้า
address têe-yòo   ที่อยู่
after lŭng   หลัง
aftershave yah tah lŭng gohn nòo-ut   ยาทาหลังโกนหนวด
again èek   อีก
air-conditioning krêu-ung air   เครื่องแอร์
airport sa-nǎhm bin   สนามบิน
alarm clock nah-li-gah bplÒOk   นาฬิกาปลุก
alcohol lâo   เหล้า
all túng mòt   ทั้งหมด
  all the streets ta-nǒn túng mòt   ถนนทั้งหมด
  that's all, thanks tâo née kòrp-kOOn   เท่านี้ขอบคุณ
almost gèu-up   เกือบ
alone kon dee-o   คนเดียว
already . . . . . . láir-o   แล้ว
always sa-mĕr   เสมอ
America a-may-ri-gah   อเมริกา
American *(adj.)* a-may-ri-gun   อเมริกัน
and láir   และ
another *(further)* èek   อีก
  (different) yàhng èun   อย่างอื่น
antibiotics yah bpùti-chee-wa-ná   ยาปฏิชีวนะ

antiseptic yah kâh chéu-a · ยาฆ่าเชื้อ

apartment a-páht-mén · อพาร์ตเม้นท์

apple aír-bpêrn · แอปเปิ้ล

arm kǎirn · แขน

arrive mah těung · มาถึง

art sǐn-la-bpà · ศิลป

ashtray têe kèe-a bOO-rèe · ที่เขี่ยบุหรี่

asleep: he's asleep káo norn lùp yòo · เขานอนหลับอยู่

at: at the coffee shop têe kórp-fêe chórp · ที่คอฟฟี่ช้อบ

attractive sǒo-ay · สวย

aunt: *(elder sister of mother or father)* bpâh · ป้า

　(younger sister of father) ah · อา

　(younger sister of mother) náh · น้า

Australia órt-sa-tray-lee-a · ออสเตรเลีย

Australian *(adj.)* órt-sa -tray-lee-a · ออสเตรเลีย

awful yâir mâhk · แย่มาก

baby dèk òrn · เด็กอ่อน

back lǔng · หลัง

backpack bpâ...y lǔng · เป้หลัง

back street ta-nǒn kâhng nai · ถนนข้างใน

bad mâi dee · ไม่ดี

baggage gra-bpǎo · กระเป๋า

baggage room têe fàhk gra-bpǎo · ที่ฝากกระเป๋า

ball lôok born · ลูกบอล

bamboo mái pài · ไม้ไผ่

bamboo shoot(s) nòr mái · หน่อไม้

banana glôo-ay — กล้วย

band (*music*) wong don-dtree — วงดนตรี

bandage pâh pun plăir — ผ้าพันแผล

  (*adhesive*) bplah-sa-dter — ปลาสเตอร์

bandit john — โจร

Bangkok grOOng-tâyp — กรุงเทพ ฯ

bank (*money*) ta-nah-kahn — ธนาคาร

bar bah — บาร์

bath àhng àhp náhm — อ่างอาบน้ำ

bathing suit chóOt àhp náhm — ชุดอาบน้ำ

bathroom hôrng náhm — ห้องน้ำ

battery bair-dta-rêe — แบตเตอรี่

beach chai-hàht — ชายหาด

beans tòo-a — ถั่ว

beard krao — เครา

beautiful (*in appearance*) sŏo-ay — สวย

because prór — เพราะ

bed dtee-ung — เตียง

bedroom hôrng norn — ห้องนอน

beef néu-a woo-a — เนื้อวัว

beer bee-a — เบียร์

before gòrn — ก่อน

beggar kŏr-tahn — ขอทาน

begin rêrm — เริ่ม

behind kâhng lŭng — ข้างหลัง

bell (*large*) ra-kung — ระฆัง

  (*small*) gra-dìng — กระดิ่ง

  (*electrical*) grìng — กริ่ง

below dtâi	ใต้
belt (*clothing*) kĕm kùt	เข็มขัด
best dee têe sòOt	ดีที่สุด
better dee gwàh	ดีกว่า
between ra-wàhng	ระหว่าง
bicycle jùk-gra-yahn	จักรยาน
big yài	ใหญ่
bikini bi-gi-nêe	บิกินี่
bill bin	บิล
birthday wun gèrt	วันเกิด
happy birthday sòOk sŭn wun gèrt	สุขสันต์วันเกิด
bitter (*taste*) kŏm	ขม
black dum	ดำ
blanket pâh hòm	ผ้าห่ม
blind dtah bòrt	ตาบอด
blinds môo-lêe	มู่ลี่
blister plăir porng	แผลพอง
blocked (*road, drain*) dtun	ตัน
blond (*adj.*) pŏm sĕe torng	ผมสีทอง
blouse sêu-a pôo-yĭng	เสื้อผู้หญิง
blue sĕe náhm ngern	สีน้ำเงิน
boat reu-a	เรือ
body râhng gai	ร่างกาย
boiled rice kâo sŏo-ay	ข้าวสวย
book (*noun*) núng-sĕu	หนังสือ
bookstore ráhn kăi núng-sĕu	ร้านขายหนังสือ
boot rorng-táo	รองเท้า
border (*of country*) chai dairn	ชายแดน

boring nâh bèu-a	น่าเบื่อ
boss jâo nai	เจ้านาย
both túng sŏrng	ทั้งสอง
bottle kòo-ut	ขวด
bottle opener têe bpèrt kòo-ut	ที่เปิดขวด
bowl chahm	ชาม
box hèep	หีบ
boxer núk moo-ay	นักมวย
boy dèk chai	เด็กชาย
boyfriend fairn	แฟน
bra sêu-a yók song	เสื้อยกทรง
bracelet gum-lai meu	กำไลมือ
brandy lâo brùn-dee	เหล้าบรั่นดี
bread ka-nŏm-bpung	ขนมปัง
breakfast ah-hăhn cháo	อาหารเช้า
bridge sa-pahn	สะพาน
briefcase gra-bpăo	กระเป๋า
British ung-grìt	อังกฤษ
broken dtàirk láir-o	แตกแล้ว
(out of order) sĕe-a	เสีย
brooch kĕm glùt sêu-a	เข็มกลัดเสื้อ
brother: older brother pêe chai	พี่ชาย
younger brother nórng chai	น้องชาย
brown sĕe náhm dtahn	สีน้ำตาล
bruise fók-chúm	ฟกช้ำ
brush *(noun)* bprairng	แปรง
Buddha prá-pÓOt-ta-jâo	พระพุทธเจ้า
building ah-kahn	อาคาร

bulb (*light*) lòrt fai fáh   หลอดไฟฟ้า
bungalow bung-gah-loh   บังกาโล
burglar ka-moy-ee   ขโมย
Burma bpra-tâyt pa-mâh   ประเทศพม่า
burn (*noun*) plǎir mâi   แผลไหม้
bus rót may   รถเมล์
business tóO-rá   ธุระ
businessman núk tóO-rá-gìt   นักธุรกิจ
bus station sa-tǎhn-ee rót may   สถานีรถเมล์
bus stop bpâi rót may   ป้ายรถเมล์
busy (*street*) jor-jair   จอแจ
  (*restaurant*) nâirn   แน่น
  (*telephone*) mâi wâhng   ไม่ว่าง
but dtàir   แต่
butter ner-ee sòt   เนยสด
button gra-dOOm   กระดุม
buy séu   ซื้อ
by: by train/car doy-ee rót fai/rót yon   ด้วยรถไฟ / รถยนต์

café ráhn gah-fair   ร้านกาแฟ
cake ka-nǒm káyk   ขนมเค้ก
calculator krêu-ung kít lâyk   เครื่องคิดเลข
call: what is this called?   นี่เรียกว่าอะไร
  nêe rêe-uk wâh a-rai?
Cambodia bpra-tâyt gum-poo-chah   ประเทศกัมพูชา
camera glôrng tài rôop   กล้องถ่ายรูป
can (*tin*) gra-bpǒrng   กระป๋อง

can: can I . . . ? pŏm (chún) . . . dâi mái?   ผม (ฉัน) ... ได้ไหม

  can you . . . ? kOOn . . . dâi mái?   คุณ ... ได้ไหม

  he can't . . . káo . . . mâi dâi   เขา ... ไม่ได้

Canada bpra-tâyt kair-nah-dah   ประเทศแคนาดา

candy tórp-fêe   ทอฟฟี่

can opener têe bpèrt gra-bpŏrng   ที่เปิดกระป๋อง

cap (hat) moo-ùk   หมวก

car rót   รถ

carbonated sâh   ซ่า

card (business) bùt   บัตร

careful: be careful ra-wung!   ระวัง

carpet prom   พรม

cash (money) ngern sòt   เงินสด

cassette móo-un tâyp kah-set   ม้วนเทปคาสเซ็ท

center (of town) jai glahng   ใจกลาง

chair gâo-êe   เก้าอี้

chambermaid yĭng rúp chái   หญิงรับใช้

change (noun: money) sàyt sa-dtahng   เศษสตางค์

  (verb: money) lâirk ngern   แลกเงิน

  (verb: clothes, trains) bplèe-un   เปลี่ยน

check chék   เช็ค

checkbook sa-mÒOt chék   สมุดเช็ค

check card bùt chék   บัตรเช็ค

cheers (toast) nothing said in Thailand

cheese ner-ee kăirng   เนยแข็ง

chess màhk róOk   หมากรุก

chest (body) nâh ok   หน้าอก

chewing gum màhk fa-rùng   หมากฝรั่ง

chicken gài   ไก่

child, children dèk   เด็ก

chili prík   พริก

China bpra-tâyt jeen   ประเทศจีน

chocolate chórk-goh-lóirt   ช็อกโกเลต

chopsticks dta-gèe-up   ตะเกียบ

church bòht   โบสถ์

cigar sí-gâh   ซิการ์

cigarette bOO-rèe   บุหรี่

city meu-ung   เมือง

clean sa-àht   สะอาด

clever cha-làht   ฉลาด

clock nah-li-gah   นาฬิกา

close: to be close (*near*) glâi   ใกล้

closed bpìt   ปิด

clothes sêu-a pâh   เสื้อผ้า

clothes hook mái nèep pâh   ไม้หนีบผ้า

coast chai ta-lay   ชายทะเล

coat (*overcoat*) sêu-a klOOm   เสื้อคลุม

  (*jacket*) sêu-a nôrk   เสื้อนอก

coathanger mái kwăirn sêu-a   ไม้แขวนเสื้อ

cockroach ma-lairng sàhp   แมลงสาบ

coconut ma-práo   มะพร้าว

coconut juice náhm ma-práo   น้ำมะพร้าว

coffee gah-fair   กาแฟ

coffee shop kórp-fêe chórp   คอฟฟี่ช้อป

cold yen   เย็น

  I have a cold pŏm (chún) bpen wùt   ผม (ฉัน) เป็นหวัด

collar bpòk kor sêu-a   ปกคอเสื้อ

color sĕe	สี
comb (noun) wĕe	หวี
come mah	มา
I come from . . . pŏm (chún) mah jàhk . . .	ผม (ฉัน) มาจาก ...
come in! chern kâo mah	เชิญเข้ามา
company (firm) bor-ri-sùt	บริษัท
complicated sùp sŏn	สับสน
computer korm-pew-dtêr	คอมพิวเตอร์
concert gahn sa-dairng don-dtree	การแสดงดนตรี
condom tŏOng yahng	ถุงยาง
constipation tórng pòok	ท้องผูก
consul gong-sŏOn	กงสุล
contact lenses korn-tàirk layn	คอนแท็คเลนซ์
cookie kóOk-gêe	คุกกี้
cool (day, weather) yen	เย็น
corner: on the corner hŏo-a mOOm	หัวมุม
in the corner yòo dtrong hŏo-a mOOm	อยู่ตรงหัวมุม
cost rah-kah	ราคา
what does it cost? rah-kah tâo-rài?	ราคาเท่าไร
cotton fâi	ฝ้าย
cotton balls sŭm-lee	สำลี
cough (verb) ai	ไอ
country (nation) bpra-tâyt	ประเทศ
cousin: my cousin yâht kŏrng pŏm (chún)	ญาติของผม (ฉัน)
crab bpoo	ปู
cramp (in leg, etc.) nèp	เหน็บ

cream kreem	ครีม
credit card bùt kray-dìt	บัตรเครดิต
crocodile jor-ra-kây	จรเข้
crowd fŏong kon	ฝูงคน
cup tôo-ay	ถ้วย
a cup of coffee gah-fair tôo-ay nèung	กาแฟถ้วยหนึ่ง
curry gairng	แกง
curtains mâhn	ม่าน
customs sŎOn-la-gah-gorn	ศุลกากร
cut dtùt	ตัด
dangerous un-dta-rai	อันตราย
dark dum	ดำ
daughter lôok săo	ลูกสาว
day wun	วัน
dead dtai	ตาย
deaf hŏo nòo-uk	หูหนวก
dear (*expensive*) pairng	แพง
deep léuk	ลึก
delicious a-ròy	อร่อย
dentist mŏr fun	หมอฟัน
deodorant yah dùp glìn dtoo-a	ยาดับกลิ่นตัว
departure kăh òrk	ขาออก
develop (*a roll of film*) láhng	ล้าง
diary sa-mÒOt bun-téuk bpra-jum wun	สมุดบันทึกประจำวัน
dictionary pót-ja-nah-nÓO-grom	พจนานุกรม
die dtai	ตาย
different dtàhng	ต่าง

difficult yâhk	ยาก	
dinner ah-hăhn yen	อาหารเย็น	
dirty sòk-ga-bpròk	สกปรก	
disabled pí-gahn	พิการ	
disco dit-sa-gôh	ดิสโก้	
divorced yàh gun láir-o	หย่ากันแล้ว	
do tum	ทำ	
doctor mŏr	หมอ	
dog măh	หมา	
dollar ngern dorn-lâh	เงินดอลล่าร์	
don't! yàh	อย่า	
door bpra-dtoo	ประตู	
down: down there yòo têe nôhn	อยู่ที่โน่น	
dress *(woman's)* sêu-a chóOt	เสื้อชุด	
drink *(verb)* dèum	ดื่ม	
drinking water náhm dèum	น้ำดื่ม	
driver's license bai kùp kèe	ใบขับขี่	
drugstore ráhn kăi yah	ร้านขายยา	
drunk mao	เมา	
dry hâirng	แห้ง	
dry-cleaner ráhn súk-hâirng	ร้านซักแห้ง	
durian *(fruit)* tóO-ree-un	ทุเรียน	
each dtàir la	แต่ละ	
ear hŏo	หู	
early *(arrive, etc.)* ray-o	เร็ว	
early in the morning cháo dtròo	เช้าตรู่	
earring dtÔOm hŏo	ตุ้มหู	
east dta-wun òrk	ตะวันออก	

easy ngâi	ง่าย
eat gin kâo	กินข้าว
egg kài	ไข่
egg noodles ba-mèe	บะหมี่
either: either . . . or . . . . . . rĕu . . .	... หรือ ...
elastic săi yahng yêut	สายยางยืด
electric fai fáh	ไฟฟ้า
electricity fai fáh	ไฟฟ้า
elephant cháhng	ช้าง
elevator líf	ลิฟท์
else: something else a-rai èek	อะไรอีก
somewhere else têe èun	ที่อื่น
embarrassing kĕrn	เขิน
embassy sa-tăhn tôot	สถานทูต
emergency chÒOk chĕrn	ฉุกเฉิน
empty *(vacant)* wâhng	ว่าง
(bottle, etc.) bplào	เปล่า
end *(verb)* sîn sÒOt, jòp	สิ้นสุด , จบ
engaged *(person)* mûn	หมั้น
England bpra-tâyt ung-grìt	ประเทศอังกฤษ
English *(adj.)* ung-grìt	อังกฤษ
(language) pah-săh ung-grìt	ภาษาอังกฤษ
enough por	พอ
entrance tahng kâo	ทางเข้า
envelope sorng jòt-măi	ซองจดหมาย
eraser yahng lóp	ยางลบ
evening dtorn glahng keun	ตอนกลางคืน
everyone tÓOk kon	ทุกคน
everything tÓOk yàhng	ทุกอย่าง

everywhere tôo-a bpai — ทั่วไป

excellent yêe-um — เยี่ยม

excuse me *(to get past)* kŏr-tôht — ขอโทษ

  (to get attention) kOOn krúp (kâ) — คุณครับ (คะ)

  excuse me? a-rai ná? — อะไรนะ

exit tahng òrk — ทางออก

expensive pairng — แพง

eye dtah — ตา

face nâh — หน้า

false teeth fun bplorm — ฟันปลอม

family krôrp-kroo-a — ครอบครัว

fan *(mechanical)* pút lom — พัดลม

  (hand-held) pút — พัด

far glai — ไกล

farmer *(of rice)* chao nah — ชาวนา

fashion fair-chûn — แฟชั่น

fast ray-o — เร็ว

fat *(person)* ôo-un — อ้วน

father pôr — พ่อ

feel róo-sèuk — รู้สึก

  I feel hot pŏm (chŭn) róo-sèuk rórn — ผม (ฉัน) รู้สึกร้อน

ferry reu-a kâhm fâhk — เรือข้ามฟาก

fever kâi — ไข้

few: only a few lék nóy — เล็กน้อย

fiancé(e) kôo mûn — คู่หมั้น

field *(rice, paddy)* nah — นา

film *(camera)* feem — ฟิล์ม

find jer — เจอ

finger néw meu   นิ้วมือ

fire: there's a fire! fai mâi!   ไฟไหม้

fire extinguisher krêu-ung dùp plerng   เครื่องดับเพลิง

first râirk   แรก

fish bplah   ปลา

fisherman kon jùp bplah   คนจับปลา

fishing jùp bplah   จับปลา

fishing boat reu-a bpra-mong   เรือประมง

flash (for camera) fláirt   แฟลช

flashlight fai chăi   ไฟฉาย

flat (adj.) bairn   แบน

flavor rót   รส

flea mùt   หมัด

flight tēe-o bin   เที่ยวบิน

flight attendant (female) "air hostess"   แอร์โฮสเตส

floating market dta-làht náhm   ตลาดน้ำ

floor (of room) péun   พื้น

flower dòrk-mái   ดอกไม้

fly (verb) bin   บิน

   (insect) ma-lairng wun   แมลงวัน

folk music don-dtree péun meu-ung   ดนตรีพื้นเมือง

food ah-hăhn   อาหาร

food poisoning ah-hăhn bpen pít   อาหารเป็นพิษ

foot táo   เท้า

for: for her sŭm-rùp káo   สำหรับเขา

   that's for me nûn sŭm-rùp
   pŏm (chún)   นั่นสำหรับผม (ฉัน)

   a bus for . . . rót-may bpai . . .   รถเมล์ไป ...

foreigner chao dtàhng bpra-tâyt   ชาวต่างประเทศ

forest bpàh	ป่า
free "free"	ฟรี
freezer dtôo châir kăirng	ตู้แช่แข็ง
French fries mun fa-rùng tôrt	มันฝรั่งทอด
fried rice kâo pùt	ข้าวผัด
friend pêu-un	เพื่อน
friendly bpen pêu-un	เป็นเพื่อน
frog gòp	กบ
from jàhk	จาก
front nâh	หน้า
fruit pŏn-la-mái	ผลไม้
fruit juice náhm pŏn-la-mái	น้ำผลไม้
fry (*deep fry*) tôrt	ทอด
(*stir fry*) pùt	ผัด
full dtem láir-o	เต็มแล้ว
I'm full pŏm (chún) ìm láir-o	ผม (ฉัน) อิ่มแล้ว
funny (*strange*) bplàirk	แปลก
(*amusing*) dta-lòk	ตลก
garbage (*waste*) ka-yà	ขยะ
garden sŏo-un	สวน
garlic gra-tee-um	กระเทียม
gas náhm mun	น้ำมัน
gas station púm náhm mun	ปั๊มน้ำมัน
gay (*homosexual*) gra-ter-ee	กระเทย
get (*fetch*) ao . . . mah	เอา ... มา
(*obtain*) dâi	ได้
(*train, bus, etc.*) kêun	ขึ้น
have you got . . . ? mee . . . mái?	มี ... ไหม

get in (*to car*) kêun   ขึ้น
  (*arrive*) mah tĕung   มาถึง
get up (*in morning*) dtèun   ตื่น
gin lâo yin   เหล้ายิน
girl pôo-yĭng   ผู้หญิง
girlfriend fairn   แฟน
give hâi   ให้
glad yin dee   ยินดี
glass gâir-o   แก้ว
glasses (*spectacles*) wâirn dtah   แว่นตา
glue gao   กาว
go bpai   ไป
gold torng   ทอง
Golden Triangle săhm lĕe-um   สามเหลี่ยมทองคำ
  torng kum
goldsmith châhng torng   ช่างทอง
good dee   ดี
good-bye lah gòrn ná   ลาก่อนนะ
government rút-ta-bahn   รัฐบาล
granddaughter lăhn săo   หลานสาว
grandfather (*paternal*) bpòo   ปู่
  (*maternal*) dtah   ตา
grandmother (*paternal*) yâh   ย่า
  (*maternal*) yai   ยาย
grandson lăhn chai   หลานชาย
grapes a-ngÒOn   องุ่น
grass yâh   หญ้า
gray sĕe tao   สีเทา

great: that's great! yôrt!   ยอด

Great Britain bpra-tâyt ung-grìt   ประเทศอังกฤษ

green sěe kěe-o   สีเขียว

ground floor chún nèung   ชั้นหนึ่ง

guide (*noun*) múk-kOO-tâyt   มัคคุเทศก์

guidebook kôo meu num têe-o   คู่มือนำเที่ยว

gun bpeun   ปืน

hair pǒm   ผม

hair dryer krêu-ung bpào pǒm   เครื่องเป่าผม

half krêung   ครึ่ง

ham mǒo hairm   หมูแฮม

hamburger hairm-ber-gêr   แฮมเบอร์เกอร์

hammer kórn   ค้อน

hand meu   มือ

handbag gra-bpǎo těu   กระเป๋าถือ

handkerchief pâh chét nâh   ผ้าเช็ดหน้า

handle (*noun*) dâhm   ด้าม

handsome rôop lòr   รูปหล่อ

hangover bpòo-ut hǒo-a   ปวดหัว

happy dee jai   ดีใจ

harbor tâh reu-a   ท่าเรือ

hard kǎirng   แข็ง

  (*difficult*) yâhk   ยาก

hat mòo-uk   หมวก

have mee   มี

  do you have . . . ? mee . . . mái?   มี ... ไหม

  I don't have . . . pǒm (chún) mâi mee . . .   ผม (ฉัน) ไม่มี ...

hay fever kâi-jahm		ไข้จาม
he káo		เขา
head hŏo-a		หัว
headache bpòo-ut hŏo-a		ปวดหัว
headlights fai nâh rót		ไฟหน้ารถ
hear dâi yin		ได้ยิน
hearing aid krêu-ung chôo-ay fung		เครื่องช่วยฟัง
heart hŏo-a jai		หัวใจ
heat kwahm rórn		ความร้อน
heavy nùk		หนัก
heel (foot) sôn táo		ส้นเท้า
(shoe) sôn rorng táo		ส้นรองเท้า
hello (said by man) sa-wùt dee krúp		สวัสดีครับ
(said by woman) sa-wùt dee kâ		สวัสดีค่ะ
help (verb) chôo-ay		ช่วย
help! chôo-ay dôo-ay!		ช่วยด้วย
her káo		เขา
her . . . . . . kŏrng káo		... ของเขา
here têe nêe		ที่นี่
hers kŏrng káo		ของเขา
hi! sa-wùt dee		สวัสดี
high sŏong		สูง
hill kăo		เขา
hill tribe chao kăo		ชาวเขา
him káo		เขา
his kŏrng káo		ของเขา
hitchhike bòhk rót		โบกรถ
holiday wun yòOt		วันหยุด

horrible yâir mâhk   แย่มาก

hostess *(in bar)* pôo-yīng bah   ผู้หญิงบาร์

hot rórn   ร้อน

  (with spices) pèt   เผ็ด

hotel rohng rairm   โรงแรม

house bâhn   บ้าน

how: how . . . ? . . . yung rai?   ... อย่างไร

hungry: I'm hungry pŏm (chún) hĕw   ผม (ฉัน) หิว

hurry: I'm in a hurry   ผม (ฉัน) ต้องรีบ
  pŏm (chún) dtôrng rêep

husband săh-mee   สามี

I *(male)* pŏm   ผม

  (female) dee-chún, chún   ดิฉัน , ฉัน

ice náhm kăirng   น้ำแข็ง

ice cream ai-sa-kreem   ไอศครีม

if tâh   ถ้า

ill mâi sa-bai   ไม่สบาย

immediately tun-tee   ทันที

impossible bpen bpai mâi dâi   เป็นไปไม่ได้

in nai   ใน

  in English bpen pah-săh ung-grìt   เป็นภาษาอังกฤษ

India bpra-tâyt in-dee-a   ประเทศอินเดีย

inexpensive tòok   ถูก

infection ah-gahn ùk-sàyp   อาการอักเสบ

information kào săhn   ข่าวสาร

insect repellent yah gun ma-lairng   ยากันแมลง

insurance bpra-gun   ประกัน

interesting nâh sŏn jai   น่าสนใจ

interpret bplair	แปล
Ireland ai-lairn	ไอร์แลนด์
iron (*for clothes*) dtao rêet	เตารีด
island gòr	เกาะ
it mun	มัน
it's expensive (mun) pairng	(มัน) แพง
jack (*for car*) mâir rairng	แม่แรง
jacket sêu-a nôrk	เสื้อนอก
jeans yeen	ยีนส์
jellyfish mairng ga-prOOn	แมงกะพรุน
jewelry pét ploy	เพชรพลอย
job ngahn	งาน
journey gahn dern tahng	การเดินทาง
jug yèu-uk	เหยือก
jungle bpàh	ป่า
junk (*boat*) reu-a sŭm-pao	เรือสำเภา
just (*only*) tâo-nún	เท่านั้น
just one un dee-o tâo-nún	อันเดียวเท่านั้น
key gOOn-jair	กุญแจ
kilo gi-loh	กิโล
kilometer gi-loh-mét	กิโลเมตร
kitchen hôrng kroo-a	ห้องครัว
knee hŏo-a kào	หัวเข่า
knife mêet	มีด
know: I don't know pŏm (chún) mâi róo	ผม (ฉัน) ไม่รู้

lady sOO-pâhp sa-dtree — สุภาพสตรี

lake ta-lay sàhp — ทะเลสาบ

lane *(narrow street)* soy — ซอย

Laos bpra-tâyt lao — ประเทศลาว

large yài — ใหญ่

last *(previous)* têe láir-o — ที่แล้ว

   (final) sÒOt-tái — สุดท้าย

   last name nahm sa-gOOn — นามสกุล

   last year bpee têe láir-o — ปีที่แล้ว

late *(at night)* dèuk — ดึก

   (behind schedule) cháh — ช้า

later tee lŭng — ทีหลัง

laundry detergent pŏng súk fôrk — ผงซักฟอก

laxative yah tài — ยาถ่าย

left *(not right)* sái — ซ้าย

leg kăh — ขา

lemon ma-nao — มะนาว

lemonade náhm ma-nao — น้ำมะนาว

letter *(in mail)* jòt-măi — จดหมาย

lettuce pùk-gàht — ผักกาด

library hôrng sa-mÒOt — ห้องสมุด

life chee-wít — ชีวิต

lift: could you give me a lift? — ช่วยไปส่งหน่อยได้ไหม
   chôo-ay bpai sòng nòy, dâi mái?

light *(noun)* fai — ไฟ

   (not heavy) bao — เบา

lighter *(cigarette)* fai cháirk — ไฟแช็ก

like: I'd like a . . . pŏm (chún) ao . . .   ผม (ฉัน) เอา ...

  I like you pŏm (chún) chôrp kOOn   ผม (ฉัน) ชอบคุณ

  one like that mĕu-un un nún   เหมือนอันนั้น

line (of people) kew   คิว

lipstick líp sa-dtík   ลิปสติก

liter lít   ลิตร

little lék   เล็ก

  just a little nít dee-o tâo-nún   นิดเดียวเท่านั้น

liver dtùp   ตับ

lobster gÔOng gâhm grahm   กุ้งก้ามกราม

long yao   ยาว

  how long does it take?   ใช้เวลานานเท่าไร
  chái way-lah nahn tâo-rài?

lose: I've lost my . . .   ... ของผม (ฉัน) หาย
  . . . kŏrng pŏm (chún) hăi

lot: a lot mâhk   มาก

  a lot of money ngern mâhk   เงินมาก

loud dung   ดัง

love: I love you chún rúk ter   ฉันรักเธอ

lovely yêe-um ler-ee   เยี่ยมเลย

low dtùm   ต่ำ

luck chôhk   โชค

  good luck! chôhk dee!   โชคดี

lunch ah-hăhn glahng wun   อาหารกลางวัน

mail jòt-măi   จดหมาย

mailbox (at a house) dtôo jòt-măi   ตู้จดหมาย

  (for mailing letters) dtôo bprai-sa-nee   ตู้ไปรษณีย์

make tum   ทำ

makeup krêu-ung sŭm-ahng   เครื่องสำอาง

man pôo-chai   ผู้ชาย

manager pôo-jùt-gahn   ผู้จัดการ

mango ma-môo-ung   มะม่วง

map păirn-têe   แผนที่

market dta-làht   ตลาด

married: I'm married pŏm (chún) dtàirng ngahn láir-o   ผม (ฉัน) แต่งงานแล้ว

massage nôo-ut   นวด

matches mái kèet   ไม้ขีด

material (*cloth*) pâh   ผ้า

me (*male*) pŏm   ผม

   (*female*) dee-chún, chún   ดิฉัน , ฉัน

  it's for me sŭm-rùp pŏm (chún)   สำหรับผม (ฉัน)

medicine yah   ยา

meeting bpra-chOOm   ประชุม

melon: watermelon dtairng moh   แตงโม

  muskmelon dtairng tai   แตงไทย

meter máyt   เมตร

middle: in the middle yòo dtrong glahng   อยู่ตรงกลาง

midnight: at midnight têe-ung keun   เที่ยงคืน

mile mai   ไมล์

milk nom   นม

mine kŏrng pŏm (chún)   ของผม (ฉัน)

mineral water náhm râe   น้ำแร่

mirror gra-jòk ngao   กระจกเงา

Miss nahng-săo   นางสาว

mistake kwahm pìt — ความผิด

monastery wút — วัด

money ngern — เงิน

monk prá — พระ

monsoon mor-ra-sŏOm — มรสุม

month deu-un — เดือน

moon prá-jun — พระจันทร์

moped rót mor-dter-sai — รถมอร์เตอร์ไซค์

more gwàh — กว่า

  more than mâhk gwàh — มากกว่า

morning cháo — เช้า

mosquito yOOng — ยุง

mosquito net mÔOng — มุ้ง

mother mâir — แม่

motorcycle rót mor-dter-sai — รถมอร์เตอร์ไซค์

mountain poo-kǎo — ภูเขา

moustache nòo-ut — หนวด

mouth bpàhk — ปาก

movie nǔng — หนัง

movie theater rohng nǔng — โรงหนัง

Mr. nai — นาย

Mrs. nahng — นาง

much mâhk — มาก

  much better dee kêun mâhk — ดีขึ้นมาก

museum pí-pít-ta-pun — พิพิธภัณฑ์

mushroom hèt — เห็ด

music don-dtree — ดนตรี

must: I must . . . pŏm (chún) dtôrng . . . — ผม (ฉัน) ต้อง ...

my . . . . . . kŏrng pŏm (chún) — ... ของผม (ฉัน)

narrow *(road)* kâirp   แคบ

near glâi   ใกล้

  is it near here? yòo glâi mái?   อยู่ใกล้ไหม

necessary jum-bpen   จำเป็น

necklace sôy kor   สร้อยคอ

need: I need a . . . pŏm (chún)   ผม (ฉัน) ต้องการ ...
  dtôrng-gahn . . .

needle kĕm   เข็ม

nephew lăhn chai   หลานชาย

never mâi ker-ee   ไม่เคย

new mài   ใหม่

news kào   ข่าว

newspaper núng-sĕu pim   หนังสือพิมพ์

New Zealand bpra-tâyt new see-láirn   ประเทศนิวซีแลนด์

next . . . . . . nâh   ... หน้า

  next to dtìt gùp   ติดกับ

nice *(person, weather)* dee   ดี

  (meal) a-ròy   อร่อย

  (town) sŏo-ay   สวย

niece lăhn săo   หลานสาว

night glahng keun   กลางคืน

  for one night keun dee-o   คืนเดียว

nightclub náit klúp   ไนท์คลับ

no *see page 10*
  I have no money pŏm (chún)   ผม (ฉัน) ไม่มีเงิน
  mâi mee ngern

noisy nòo-uk hŏo   หนวกหู

noodles gŏo-ay dtĕe-o   ก๋วยเตี๋ยว

  fried noodles *(Thai-style)* pùt tai   ผัดไทย

noodle shop ráhn gŏo-ay dtĕe-o   ร้านก๋วยเตี๋ยว

noon: at noon têe-ung wun   เที่ยงวัน

north nĕu-a   เหนือ

nose ja-mòok   จมูก

not mâi   ไม่

  not for me mâi châi sŭm-rùp   ไม่ใช่สำหรับผม (ฉัน)
  pŏm (chún)

nothing mâi mee a-rai   ไม่มีอะไร

now dĕe-o née   เดี๋ยวนี้

number (*figure*) măi lâyk   หมายเลข

  (*room*) ber hôrng   เบอร์ห้อง

  (*telephone*) ber toh-ra-sùp   เบอร์โทรศัพท์

of kŏrng   ของ

  the name of the hotel   ชื่อของโรงแรม
  chêu kŏrng rohng rairm

office têe tum ngahn   ที่ทำงาน

often bòy bòy   บ่อย ๆ

oil (*motor*) náhm mun krêu-ung   น้ำมันเครื่อง

  (*vegetable*) náhm mun pêut   น้ำมันพืช

OK oh-kay   โอเค

old (*things*) gào   เก่า

  (*people*) gàir   แก่

on bon   บน

  on the beach chai ta-lay   ชายทะเล

  on the roof bon lŭng-kah   บนหลังคา

one nèung   หนึ่ง

  that one un nún   อันนั้น

onion hŏo-a hŏrm   หัวหอม

only . . . . . . tâo-nún	... เท่านั้น
open (adj.) bpèrt	เปิด
opposite: opposite the temple dtrong kâhm wút	ตรงข้ามวัด
or rĕu	หรือ
orange (fruit) sôm	ส้ม
(color) sĕe sôm	สีส้ม
orange juice náhm sôm	น้ำส้ม
other: the other . . . èek . . . nèung	อีก ... หนึ่ง
our(s) . . . . . . kŏrng rao	... ของเรา
out: he's out káo mâi yòo	เขาไม่อยู่
outside kâhng nôrk	ข้างนอก
over: over there têe nôhn	ที่โน่น
oyster hŏy nahng rom	หอยนางรม

package hòr	ห่อ
packet sorng	ซอง
paddy field nah	นา
page (of book) nâh	หน้า
pair kôo	คู่
pajamas sêu-a gahng-gayng norn	เสื้อกางเกงนอน
pants gahng-gayng	กางเกง
paper gra-dàht	กระดาษ
parents pôr-mâir	พ่อแม่
park (noun) sŏo-un săh-tah-ra-ná	สวนสาธารณะ
(verb) jòrt	จอด
parking lot têe jòrt rót	ที่จอดรถ
party (group) glÒOm kon	กลุ่มคน
(celebration) ngahn lée-ung	งานเลี้ยง

passport núng-sĕu dern tahng   หนังสือเดินทาง

path tahng   ทาง

pay *(verb)* jài   จ่าย

  can I pay, please? chôo-ay gèp dtung nòy   ช่วยเก็บสตางค์หน่อย

pen bpàhk-gah   ปากกา

pencil din-sŏr   ดินสอ

people kon   คน

pepper *(spice)* prík tai   พริกไทย

  green pepper prík yòo-uk   พริกหยวก

  red pepper prík yòo-uk dairng   พริกหยวกแดง

per: . . . per night keun la . . .   คืนละ ...

perfume náhm hŏrm   น้ำหอม

perhaps bahng tee   บางที

perm dùt pŏm   ดัดผม

person kon   คน

photograph *(noun)* rôop tài   รูปถ่าย

  (verb) tài rôop   ถ่ายรูป

photographer châhng tài rôop   ช่างถ่ายรูป

phrase book kôo meu sŏn-ta-nah   คู่มือสนทนา

pickpocket ka-moy-ee lóo-ung gra-bpăo   โขมยล้วงกระเป๋า

picture rôop   รูป

piece chín   ชิ้น

  a piece of . . . . . . chín nèung   ... ชิ้นหนึ่ง

pillow mŏrn   หมอน

pin *(noun)* kĕm mÒOt   เข็มหมุด

pineapple sùp-bpa-rót   สับปะรด

pink sĕe chom-poo   สีชมพู

pipe (*smoking*) glôrng yah sòop   กล้องยาสูบ
  (*water*) tôr náhm   ท่อน้ำ

place (*noun*) sa-tăhn-têe   สถานที่

plane krêu-ung bin   เครื่องบิน

plant dtôn mái   ต้นไม้

plastic bag tŏOng bplah-sa-tìk   ถุงพลาสติก

plate jahn   จาน

play (*in theater*) la-korn   ละคร

please: yes, please dee see krúp (kâ)   ดีซิครับ (ค่ะ)
  could you please . . . ?   ช่วย ... หน่อยได้ไหม
  chôo-ay . . . nòy dâi mái?

plug bplúk   ปลั๊ก

pocket gra-bpăo   กระเป๋า

pocketknife mêet púp   มีดพับ

poisonous bpen pít   เป็นพิษ

police dtum-ròo-ut   ตำรวจ

police officer dtum ròo-ut   ตำรวจ

polite sOO-pâhp   สุภาพ

pool (*for swimming*) sà wâi náhm   สระว่ายน้ำ

poor (*not rich*) jon   จน

pop music playng bpórp   เพลงป๊อป

poppy dòrk fìn   ดอกฝิ่น

pork néu-a mŏo   เนื้อหมู

porter (*hotel*) kon fâo bpra-dtoo   คนเฝ้าประตู
  (*station, etc.*) pa-núk ngahn rót fai   พนักงานรถไฟ

possible bpen bpai dâi   เป็นไปได้

post (*noun: mail*) jòt-măi   จดหมาย

postcard bpóht-káht   โปสการ์ด

post office bprai-sa-nee   ไปรษณีย์

potato mun fa-rùng   มันฝรั่ง

potato chips mun fa-rùng tôrt   มันฝรั่งทอด

prawns gÔÔng   กุ้ง

pregnant mee tórng   มีท้อง

present (*gift*) kŏrng kwŭn   ของขวัญ

pretty sŏo-ay   สวย

price rah-kah   ราคา

priest prá   พระ

problem bpun-hăh   ปัญหา

prostitute sŏh-pay-nee   โสเภณี

pull deung   ดึง

puncture yahng dtàirk   ยางแตก

purse (*for money*) gra-bpăo sa-dtahng   กระเป๋าสตางค์

push plùk   ผลัก

question kum tăhm   คำถาม

quick ray-o   เร็ว

quiet (*place, hotel*) ngêe-up   เงียบ

quite: quite a lot mâhk por   มากพอสมควร
  sŏm-koo-un

radiator môr náhm   หม้อน้ำ

radio wít-ta-yÓÓ   วิทยุ

railroad tahng rót fai   ทางรถไฟ

rain (*noun*) fŏn   ฝน

  it's raining fŏn dtòk   ฝนตก

rainy season nâh fŏn   หน้าฝน

rat nŏo   หนู

razor mêet gohn   มีดโกน

razor blades bai mêet gohn	ใบมีดโกน
read àhn	อ่าน
ready (*finished*) sèt	เสร็จ
receipt bai sèt rúp ngern	ใบเสร็จรับเงิน
record (*music*) jahn sěe-ung	จานเสียง
red sěe dairng	สีแดง
refrigerator dtôo yen	ตู้เย็น
religion sǎh-sa-nǎh	ศาสนา
rent (*for room, etc.*) kâh châo	ค่าเช่า
(*verb: car, etc.*) châo	เช่า
repair (*verb*) sôrm	ซ่อม
reserve jorng	จอง
restaurant ráhn ah-hǎhn	ร้านอาหาร
restroom (*men's*) hôrng náhm pôo-chai	ห้องน้ำผู้ชาย
(*women's*) hôrng náhm pôo-yǐng	ห้องน้ำผู้หญิง
return (*come back*) glùp	กลับ
(*give back*) keun hâi	คืนให้
rice kâo	ข้าว
rice field nah	นา
rich (*person*) roo-ay	รวย
right (*correct*) tòok	ถูก
(*not left*) kwǎh	ขวา
ring (*on finger*) wǎirn	แหวน
river mâir náhm	แม่น้ำ
road ta-nǒn	ถนน
roof lǔng-kah	หลังคา
room hôrng	ห้อง
(*space*) têe wâhng	ที่ว่าง
rope chêu-uk	เชือก

round (*adj.*) glom | กลม

  it's my round bpen tee kŏrng pŏm (chún) | เป็นที่ของผม (ฉัน)

round-trip ticket dtŏo-a bpai-glùp | ตั๋วไปกลับ

rubber (*material*) yahng | ยาง

rubber band yahng rút | ยางรัด

ruins sâhk sa-lùk hùk pung | ซากสลักหักพัง

rum lâo rum | เหล้ารัม

run (*person*) wîng | วิ่ง

sad sâo | เศร้า

safe (*not in danger*) bplòrt-pai | ปลอดภัย

  (*not dangerous*) mâi un-dta-rai | ไม่อันตราย

safety pin kěm glùt | เข็มกลัด

salad sa-lùt | สลัด

salt gleu-a | เกลือ

same měu-un gun | เหมือนกัน

  the same again, please kŏr yàhng derm | ขออย่างเดิม

sampan (*type of boat*) reu-a sŭm-bpûn | เรือสำปั้น

sand sai | ทราย

sandal(s) rorng táo dtàir | รองเท้าแตะ

sandwich sairn-wít | แซนด์วิช

sanitary napkins pâh a-nah-mai | ผ้าอนามัย

sauce náhm jîm | น้ำจิ้ม

sausage sâi gròrk | ไส้กรอก

say: how do you say . . . in Thai? . . . pah-săh tai pôot wâh yung-rai? | ... ภาษาไทยพูดว่าอย่างไร

school rohng ree-un | โรงเรียน

scissors dta-grai | ตะไกร

Scotland bpra-tâyt sa-górt-lairn	ประเทศสกอตแลนด์
screwdriver kăi koo-ung	ไขควง
sea ta-lay	ทะเล
seafood ah-hăhn ta-lay	อาหารทะเล
seat têe nûng	ที่นั่ง
seat belt kĕm kùt ni-ra-pai	เข็มขัดนิรภัย
second (in series) têe sŏrng	ที่สอง
(of time) wí-nah-tee	วินาที
see hĕn	เห็น
I see! kâo jai láir-o	เข้าใจแล้ว
sell kăi	ขาย
separately (pay, travel) yâirk gun	แยกกัน
sew yép	เย็บ
shade: in the shade nai rôm	ในร่ม
shampoo yah sà pŏm	ยาสระผม
shark bplah cha-lăhm	ปลาฉลาม
shave gohn	โกน
shaving cream kreem gohn nòo-ut	ครีมโกนหนวด
she káo	เขา
sheet (for bed) pâh bpoo têe norn	ผ้าปูที่นอน
ship reu-a	เรือ
shirt sêu-a chért	เสื้อเชิ้ต
shoe rorng táo	รองเท้า
shoelaces chêu-uk pòok rorng táo	เชือกผูกรองเท้า
shop ráhn	ร้าน
short (in length) sûn	สั้น
(person) dtêe-a	เตี้ย
shorts gahng-gayng kăh sûn	กางเกงขาสั้น
shoulder lài	ไหล่

shower (in bathroom) fùk boo-a   ฝักบัว

shrimp gÔOng   กุ้ง

shut (verb) bpìt   ปิด

shutter (on window) sa-lùk nâh-dtàhng   สลักหน้าต่าง

sick (ill) mâi sa-bai   ไม่สบาย

side street soy   ซอย

sidewalk bàht wít-těe   บาทวิถี

sight: the sights of . . . sa-tǎhn-têe   สถานที่น่าเที่ยวใน ...
  nâh têe-o nai . . .

silk mǎi   ไหม

silver ngern   เงิน

sing rórng playng   ร้องเพลง

single: I'm single pǒm (chún)   ผม (ฉัน) เป็นโสด
  bpen sòht

sister: older sister pêe sǎo   พี่สาว

  younger sister nórng sǎo   น้องสาว

sit nûng   นั่ง

skirt gra-bprohng   กระโปรง

sky fáh   ฟ้า

sleep norn lùp   นอนหลับ

slow cháh   ช้า

slowly cháh cháh   ช้า ๆ

small lék   เล็ก

smell (have bad smell) měn   เหม็น

smile (verb) yím   ยิ้ม

smoke (noun) kwun   ควัน

  do you smoke? kOOn sòop   คุณสูบบุหรี่ไหม
  bOO-rèe mái?

snake ngoo   งู

so: **so good** dee jing	ดีจริง
not so much mâi mâhk tâo-rài	ไม่มากเท่าไร
soap sa-bòo	สบู่
soccer fóOt-born	ฟุตบอล
sock tŏOng-táo	ถุงเท้า
soft (*material, etc.*) nîm	นิ่ม
soft drink náhm kòo-ut	น้ำขวด
sole (*of shoes*) péun rorng táo	พื้นรองเท้า
somebody krai	ใคร
something a-rai	อะไร
sometimes bahng tee	บางที
somewhere têe năi	ที่ไหน
son lôok chai	ลูกชาย
song playng	เพลง
soon dĕe-o	เดี๋ยว
sorry kŏr-tôht	ขอโทษ
sorry? a-rai ná krúp (ká)?	อะไรนะครับ (คะ)
soup sóOp	ซุบ
south dtâi	ใต้
souvenir kŏrng têe ra-léuk	ของที่ระลึก
soy sauce náhm see éw	น้ำซีอิ๋ว
spark plug hŏo-a tee-un	หัวเทียน
speak pôot	พูด
spider mairng mOOm	แมงมุม
spoon chórn	ช้อน
spring (*season*) reu-doo bai mái plì	ฤดูใบไม้ผลิ
squid bplah-mèuk	ปลาหมึก
stairs bun-dai	บันได
stamp (*for letter*) sa-dtairm	แสตมป์

119

start (*noun*) rêrm	เริ่ม
station (*train*) sa-tǎhn-nee rót fai	สถานีรถไฟ
steak néu-a sa-dték	เนื้อเสต็ก
steal: my bag has been stolen gra-bpǎo tòok ka-moy-ee	กระเป๋าถูกขโมย
sticky rice kâo něe-o	ข้าวเหนียว
stockings tǒong nôrng	ถุงน่อง
stomach tórng	ท้อง
stop (*bus stop*) bpâi rót-may	ป้ายรถเมล์
stop here yòot têe nêe	หยุดที่นี่
storm pah-yóo	พายุ
straight: it's straight ahead yòo dtrong nâh	อยู่ตรงหน้า
street ta-nǒn	ถนน
string chêu-uk	เชือก
student núk sèuk-sǎh	นักศึกษา
stupid ngôh	โง่
sugar náhm dtahn	น้ำตาล
suit (*noun*) chóot	ชุด
suitcase gra-bpǎo dern tahng	กระเป๋าเดินทาง
sun prá-ah-tít	พระอาทิตย์
sunblock (*cream*) yah tah gun dàirt	ยาทากันแดด
sunburn mâi dàirt	ไหม้แดด
sunburned tòok dàirt	ถูกแดด
sunglasses wâirn gun dàirt	แว่นกันแดด
sunshade rôm gun dàirt	ร่มกันแดด
sunstroke rôhk páir dàirt	โรคแพ้แดด
suntan pěw klúm dàirt	ผิวคล้ำแดด
suntan lotion kreem tah àhp dàirt	ครีมทาอาบแดด

supermarket sÓO-bpêr-mah-gêt   ซุปเปอร์มาร์เก็ต

sure: I'm sure pŏm (chún) nâir jai   ผม (ฉัน) แน่ใจ

  are you sure? kOOn nâir jai rĕu?   คุณแน่ใจหรือ

swamp nŏrng náhm   หนองน้ำ

sweat (*noun*) ngèu-a   เหงื่อ

  (*verb*) ngèu-a òrk   เหงื่อออก

sweater sêu-a sa-wét-dtêr   เสื้อเสวตเตอร์

sweet (*taste*) wăhn   หวาน

sweet and sour bprêe-o wăhn   เปรี้ยวหวาน

sweltering: it's sweltering   ร้อนเป็นบ้า
  rórn bpen bâh

swim (*verb*) wâi náhm   ว่ายน้ำ

swimming pool sà wâi náhm   สระว่ายน้ำ

swimming trunks   กางเกงว่ายน้ำ
  gahng gayng wâi náhm

swollen boo-um   บวม

table dtó   โต๊ะ

take (*something somewhere*) ao . . . bpai   เอา ... ไป

  (*someone somewhere*) pah . . . bpai   พา ... ไป

talk (*verb*) pôot   พูด

tall sŏong   สูง

tampons tairm-porn   แทมพอน

tap górk náhm   ก๊อกน้ำ

tape táyp   เทป

  (*adhesive, invisible*) sa-górt táyp   สก๊อตเทป

taxi táirk-sêe   แท็กซี่

tea náhm chah   น้ำชา

telegram toh-ra-lâyk   โทรเลข

telephone toh-ra-sùp   โทรศัพท์

television toh-ra-tút   โทรทัศน์

temperature (*weather*) OOn-na-ha-poom   อุณหภูมิ
  (*fever*) kâi   ไข้

temple (*religious*) wút   วัด

tent tén   เต็นท์

terrible yâir mâhk   แย่มาก

Thai (*adj.*) tai   ไทย
  (*language*) pah-sǎh tai   ภาษาไทย

Thailand (*formal word*) bpra-tâyt tai   ประเทศไทย
  (*informal word*) meu-ung tai   เมืองไทย

than gwàh   กว่า
  smaller than . . . lék gwàh . . .   เล็กกว่า ...

thanks, thank you kòrp-kOOn   ขอบคุณ

that: that woman pôo-yǐng kon nún   ผู้หญิงคนนั้น
  that man pôo chai kon nún   ผู้ชายคนนั้น
  what's that? nûn a-rai?   นั่นอะไร

the *no articles in Thai*

theater rohng la-korn   โรงละคร

their . . . . . . kǒrng káo   ... ของเขา

theirs kǒrng káo   ของเขา

them káo   เขา

then (*after that*) lǔng jàhk nún   หลังจากนั้น
  (*at that time*) way-lah nún   เวลานั้น

there têe-nûn   ที่นั่น
  is/are there . . . ? mee . . . mái?   มี ... ไหม
  there is/are . . . mee . . .   มี ...
  there isn't/ aren't . . . mâi mee . . .   ไม่มี ...

these pôo-uk née   พวกนี้

they *(people)* káo · เขา

  (things) mun · มัน

thick năh · หนา

thin bahng · บาง

thing kŏrng · ของ

think kít · คิด

thirsty: I'm thirsty pŏm (chún) hĕw náhm · ผม (ฉัน) หิวน้ำ

this: this street ta-nŏn née · ถนนนี้

  this one un née · อันนี้

  what's this? nêe a-rai? · นี่อะไร

those pôo-uk nún · พวกนั้น

throat kor · คอ

through pàhn · ผ่าน

thunderstorm pah-yóo fŏn · พายุฝน

ticket dtŏo-a · ตั๋ว

tie *(around neck)* nék-tai · เน็คไท

tights tŏong yai boo-a · ถุงใยบัว

time way-lah · เวลา

  what's the time? gèe mohng láir-o? · กี่โมงแล้ว

  next time krao nâh · คราวหน้า

timetable dtah-rahng way-lah · ตารางเวลา

tip *(money)* ngern típ · เงินทิป

tire yahng rót · ยางรถ

tired nèu-ay · เหนื่อย

tissues pâh chét meu · ผ้าเช็ดมือ

to: to England bpai ung-grìt · ไปอังกฤษ

toast *(bread)* ka-nŏm bpung bpîng · ขนมปังปิ้ง

toasted bananas glôo-ay bpîng · กล้วยปิ้ง

today wun née   วันนี้

together dôo-ay gun   ด้วยกัน

toilet hôrng náhm   ห้องน้ำ

toilet paper gra-dàht chum-rá   กระดาษชำระ

tomato ma-kĕu-a tâyt   มะเขือเทศ

tomato juice náhm ma-kĕu-a tâyt   น้ำมะเขือเทศ

tomorrow prôOng née   พรุ่งนี้

tonic (*water*) náhm toh-ník   น้ำโทนิค

tonight keun née   คืนนี้

too (*excessively*) . . . . . . gern bpai   ... เกินไป
   (*also*) dôo-ay   ด้วย

tooth fun   ฟัน

toothbrush bprairng sĕe fun   แปรงสีฟัน

toothpaste yah sĕe fun   ยาสีฟัน

tour (*noun*) rai-gahn num têe-o   รายการนำเที่ยว

tourist núk tôrng têe-o   นักท่องเที่ยว

tourist office sŭm-núk ngahn gahn   สำนักงานการท่องเที่ยว
   tôrng têe-o

towel pâh chét dtoo-a   ผ้าเช็ดตัว

town meu-ung   เมือง

traffic lights fai sŭn-yahn ja-rah-jorn   ไฟสัญญาณจราจร

train rót fai   รถไฟ

translate bplair   แปล

travel agent bor-ri-sùt num têe-o   บริษัทนำเที่ยว

traveler's check chék dern tahng   เช็คเดินทาง

tree dtôn mái   ต้นไม้

try (*try out, test*) lorng   ลอง

T-shirt sêu-a yêut   เสื้อยืด

tweezers bpàhk kêep   ปากคีบ

umbrella rôm   ร่ม

uncle (*older brother of father
or mother*) lOOng   ลุง

  (*younger brother of father*) ah   อา

  (*younger brother of mother*) náh   น้า

under (*spatially*) dtâi   ใต้

vaccination chéet wúk seen   ฉีดวัคซีน

vanilla wá-ní-lah   วานิลา

vase jair-gun   แจกัน

vegetables pùk   ผัก

vegetarian mâi gin néu-a   ไม่กินเนื้อ

very . . . . . . mâhk   ... มาก

village mòo-bâhn   หมู่บ้าน

visa wee-sâh   วีซ่า

visit (*places*) têe-o   เที่ยว

  (*people*) yêe-um   เยี่ยม

vodka word-gâh   วอดก้า

voice sĕe-ung   เสียง

voltage rairng fai fáh   แรงไฟฟ้า

wait ror   รอ

waiter kon sèrp   คนเสริฟ

waitress kon sèrp yĭng   คนเสริฟหญิง

Wales "Wales"   เวลส์

wall (*inside*) făh   ฝา

  (*outside*) gum-pairng   กำแพง

wallet gra-bpăo sa-dtahng   กระเป๋าสตางค์

warm òp ÒOn   อบอุ่น

wasp dtairn — แตน

watch (*wrist-*) nah-li-gah kôr meu — นาฬิกาข้อมือ

water náhm — น้ำ

we rao — เรา

weather ah-gàht — อากาศ

wedding pi-tee dtàirng ngahn — พิธีแต่งงาน

week ah-tít — อาทิตย์

welcome: you're welcome — ไม่เป็นไร
  mâi bpen rai

west dta-wun dtòk — ตะวันตก

wet bpèe-uk — เปียก

what a-rai? — อะไร

wheel lór — ล้อ

when? mêu-a rai? — เมื่อไร

where? têe năi? — ที่ไหน

  where is . . . ? . . . yòo têe năi? — ... อยู่ที่ไหน

which: which one? un năi? — อันไหน

whiskey wít-sa-gêe — วิสกี้

white sĕe kăo — สีขาว

who? krai? — ใคร

why? tum-mai? — ทำไม

wide gwâhng — กว้าง

wife pun-ra-yah — ภรรยา

wind (*noun*) lom — ลม

window nâh-dtàhng — หน้าต่าง

wine lâo a-ngÒOn — เหล้าองุ่น

with gùp — กับ

without mâi sài — ไม่ใส่

woman pôo-yĭng — ผู้หญิง